Blood Over Texas

Blood Over Texas

Sanford H. Montaigne

ARLINGTON HOUSE·PUBLISHERS
NEW ROCHELLE, NEW YORK

Manufactured in the United States of America

Library of Congress Cataloging in Publication Data

Montaigne, Sanford H.
    Blood over Texas.

    Bibliography: p.
    Includes index.
    1. United States—History—War with Mexico, 1845-1848—Causes. 2. Texas-
—History—To 1846. I. Title. E407.M66   973.6'21   75-28056
ISBN 0-87000-342-9

To Ginny

CONTENTS

Acknowledgments

This investigation into the founding of the Texas Republic and the origins of the Mexican War is based on research into primary sources, the vast majority of which are located in the Latin American Collection of the University of Texas Library. I wish to thank most sincerely Miss Laura Gutiérrez, Assistant Librarian, who permitted me use of the facilities of this collection and who was most helpful in deciphering many difficult words. In addition to Miss Gutiérrez her staff, consisting of Mrs. Wanda Turnley (Senior Library Assistant) and Miss Carmen Cobas (Library Assistant) was most helpful.

Many other useful primary sources were located in the Barker Texas History Center of the University of Texas Library. For permission to use these facilities I would like to thank Dr. Chester V. Kielman, the director and chief archivist. I also wish to thank Dr. Kielman's assistant, Robert W. Tissing, Jr., who was most cooperative in helping me locate many items.

I should also like to single out my good friend and fellow historian, Joseph D. O'Brien, who patiently listened to my thesis unfold and who made many helpful suggestions. Finally, to everyone at the University of Texas, Temple University, and the University of Pennsylvania who helped me, I express my heartfelt appreciation.

Introduction

Revisionist historians have portrayed America as an imperialist power, responsible for starting the Cold War against Stalinist Russia, slaughtering native Indian innocents, and bullying our Latin American neighbors. The multitude of charges are ingenious, varied, and sometimes entertaining. The pleasure derived is apparently similar to that which some persons enjoy from seeing the biggest boy on the block take his licks.

A certain segment of the American community seems to derive inordinate pleasure from the self-flagellation of revisionist history, the role reversal that makes the cowboys the bad guys and the Indians the saints . . . as if there weren't always saints and sinners on both sides. But today the significant issues are all too frequently overlooked. In its development and dealings with other nations, was the American record worse or better than that of other nations? Did we exercise more restraint, or less, than was the norm in dealing with political provocations? Was America a blundering giant or a normally developing society in the mid-19th century?

Aside from our dealings with American Indian tribes, the

earliest case of clear American "imperialism" cited is usually the Mexican War of 1846. A controversial struggle in its own time, the revisionists have found ample material available to paint the portrait of imperialistic, cruel Americans seeking *lebensraum* at the expense of peace-loving Mexico. The only difficulty is that the facts do not always support the image, which is the reason that facts are frequently discarded or ignored in the lecture halls of many colleges, in textbooks, and in the popular fiction that now passes for American history.

This book is an attempt to right the record of the Mexican War, to show where the burden of responsibility fell, and why. This is not an anti-Mexican book any more than those works that place the primary responsibility for the war on this country are necessarily anti-American. It is, however, a response to a distortion of this country's history, which together with other misinterpretations has tarnished our image and misled millions of young Americans into believing that America is among the most venal of nations. Like that of all great countries, our record in dealing with others is open to criticism, but on balance it will compare favorably with the records of its contemporaries.

At issue in 1846 were two fundamentally conflicting views of the status of the former Republic of Texas. The Mexican view was that Texas, which had gained its independence in 1836, was still an integral part of Mexico. The prevailing view in Washington, held by both President James K. Polk and the majority in Congress, was that Texas had become an independent country with the right to chart the course of its own destiny. This Texas had done when it elected to join the United States.

A secondary Mexican contention was that the southern border of Texas was formed by the Nueces River. The contrary view, long held by the Texan government that was actually in control of the disputed territory, was that the border was formed by the Rio Grande. The latter position was supported by the American government.

On May 11, 1846 President Polk sent to Congress his message asking for a declaration of war against Mexico. In his message the President stressed the fact that Mexico had committed an act of hostility against the American army under the command of General Zachary Taylor. The Mexicans, under General Mariano Arista's command, had attacked General Taylor's troops in the state of Texas, and "American blood had been shed upon American soil."

President Polk reacted to this first attack on American forces by a foreign power since the War of 1812 with these words:

> . . . after reiterated menaces, Mexico has passed the boundary of the United States, has invaded our territory and shed American blood upon American soil. She has proclaimed that hostilities have commenced, and that the two nations are now at war.

President Polk continued:

> As war exists, and notwithstanding all our efforts to avoid it, exists by the act of Mexico herself, we are called upon by every consideration of duty and patriotism to vindicate with decision the honor, the rights, and the interests of our country.[1]

President Mariano Paredes y Arrillaga of Mexico denied that Texas was a part of the United States. President Paredes stated:

> The Mexican republic, despoiled of the rich, extensive territory of Texas, which has always belonged to her, by direct acts of the supreme authority of the neighboring republic [United States], discovered the designs of the latter to take over some others of our border Departments; the Mexican nation ought to have protested, has protested, and now I protest solemnly in her name, that she does not recognize the American flag on the soil of Texas, that she will defend her invaded property and will nevermore permit new conquests or new advances from the government of the United States of America.[2]

[1]James D. Richardson (Ed.), *A Compilation of the Messages and Papers of the Presidents, 1789-1897* (20 vols., New York: Bureau of National Literature, 1897), VI, 2292. In an alternate edition, published in Washington by the Government Printing Office in 1897, the citation would be IV, 442. Hereafter cited as Richardson, *Messages of the Presidents*.

[2]Mariano Paredes y Arrillaga to the people of Mexico, Mar. 21, 1846, in Mexico, Executive Document, *Ultimas Comunicaciónes entre el Gobierno Mexicano y el enviado estraordinario y ministro plenipotenciario nombrado por el de los Estados Unidos, sobre la Cuestión De Tejas, y admisión de dicho agente* (Mexico City: Imprenta de Ignacio Cumplido, 1846), p. 4. Paredes Papers, Garcia Collection, University of Texas Archives, Latin American Collection, Austin, Texas.

While Paredes mentions that Mexico has discovered the designs of the United States to take over other border departments of his nation, he does not, it should be noted, cite any particular design or identify any particular department.

Furthermore, a future American President, Abraham Lincoln, then an Illinois congressman, denied that "American blood had been shed upon American soil." In his famous "Spot Resolutions" on December 22, 1847, Congressman Lincoln queried President Polk about the spot where "American blood had been shed upon American soil." The following month, on January 12, 1848 Lincoln took President Polk to task concerning the commencement of the war (then in progress) in general and the southwestern boundary of Texas in particular.

The spot, of course, was in Texas, which had entered the American Union on December 29, 1845. President Polk, in his war message of May 11, 1846, had pointed out that Congress had recognized the area between the Nueces River and the Rio Grande, where the actual bloodshed had occurred, as part of the United States. President Polk had also mentioned that the Congress of Texas, in its act of December 19, 1836, had declared the Rio Grande to be the boundary of that republic. The jurisdiction of the Republic of Texas, President Polk explained, "had been extended and exercised beyond the Nueces." Furthermore, the territory between the Nueces and the Rio Grande had been represented in the Texan Congress and in the Texan convention that had voted in favor of annexation to the United States. Finally, President Polk stated, the Congress of the United States had with great unanimity, on December 31, 1845, "recognized the country beyond the Nueces as a part of our territory by including it within our own revenue system, and a revenue officer to reside within that district has been appointed by and with the advice and consent of the Senate."[3]

On April 12, 1846 General Pedro de Ampudia, the top-ranking Mexican general on the frontier, assumed a belligerent attitude and ordered General Zachary Taylor, his American counterpart, "to break up his camp within twenty-four hours

[3]Richardson, *Messages of the Presidents*, VI, 2290 (or IV, 440).

and to retire beyond the Nueces River." In the event that General Taylor should disobey the ultimatum, Ampudia threatened that "arms, and arms alone, must decide the question."[4]

It was not until April 24, however, that an open act of hostility was actually committed. On that date, General Mariano Arista, who had succeeded General Ampudia as commander of the Mexican army of invasion that very day, notified General Taylor that "he considered hostilities commenced and should prosecute them"[5] Taylor responded by informing Arista that the responsibility for beginning a war must rest with those who actually fire the first shot.

The next day, General Anastasio Torrejón, who had crossed the Rio Grande and thus had invaded Texas on the 24th under orders from General Arista, attacked an American reconnoitering party of 63 dragoons under the command of Captain Seth Thornton. After 11 of the Americans were killed, the rest were forced to surrender. The Mexican invasion force numbered 1600 cavalry.

General Arista later declared, in December of 1847: "I had the pleasure of being the first to begin the war."[6]

Various Interpretations Explored

This book represents a new interpretation of the Mexican War to the effect that that war was an outgrowth of the Texan War of Independence, which in turn stemmed from the disinclination of Mexican federalists, including the Texans, to accept the overthrow of the Mexican federal constitution of 1824 by an adventurer–turned–dictator, General Antonio López de Santa Anna.

[4]*Ibid.*, VI, 2291 (or IV, 441).

[5]*Ibid.*

[6]Justin Harvey Smith, *The War with Mexico*, (2 vols.; New York: Macmillan, 1919), I, 155. Hereafter cited as Smith, *The War with Mexico*.

At this juncture a synopsis of various other historical interpretations regarding the causes of the Mexican War will be presented.

1. The Slave Power Conspiracy. One of the earliest theories concerning the causes of the Mexican War was that of James Ford Rhodes. Rhodes and others who adhered to this school of thought believed that the Southern slaveocracy, in its desire to acquire more land for slavery, was responsible for the Mexican War.

2. Western Responsibility. William E. Dodd expounded the view that the West, rather than the South, was responsible for the Mexican War. In Dodd's view, President James Knox Polk was a "Westerner" rather than a "Southerner." The forces that helped nominate and elect Polk were the same that had earlier supported President Andrew Jackson, Polk's fellow Tennessean and an earlier "Western" leader. Even Senator Robert J. Walker of Mississippi, later Polk's Secretary of the Treasury, is seen as a "Western" rather than a "Southern" expansionist.

3. Manifest Destiny. Both the Southern slave power conspiracy theory and the Western drive for more land theory might be considered as segments of yet a third thesis: that of Manifest Destiny. Albert K. Weinberg, a leading exponent of the Manifest Destiny theory, blamed American imperialism for the Mexican War. According to this interpretation, Americans felt it was their destiny to expand the frontiers of American democracy. Here American expansion is seen as a providential mission on a national basis rather than as merely a desire for sectional aggrandizement.

4. Mercantile Theory. Norman A. Graebner challenges the land-hunger thesis, whether of the South or the West. Furthermore, Graebner believes that Manifest Destiny is a broad generalization that does not bear close scrutiny. According to Graebner's mercantile theory, westward expansion reflected the views of commercial groups that coveted ports and waterways on the Pacific.

5. Polk's Responsibility. One of the more famous exponents of the "Blame Polk" school is Richard R. Stenberg. According to this theory, President Polk relied on a policy of expansion by covert aggression. Stenberg depicts Polk as an intriguer who provoked Mexico into initiating hostilities.

6. An American Plot. Closely related to the five mentioned theories—all of which blame the United States for the Mexican War—are the views of Hubert H. Bancroft. The emphasis here is on Mexico as the "innocent victim" of American aggression. Bancroft's views, rather than representing a distinct school or interpretation, might be seen as an eclectic combination of theories that blame the United States. Whereas the Manifest Destiny school cloaks the other contentions blaming the United States for the Mexican War under the mantle of a desire to expand American democracy, Bancroft removes this covering and excoriates the alleged machinations of the imperialistic slaveocracy and the insatiable land greed of the West.

Bancroft's thesis, incidentally, is the one that most nearly voices the views of most Mexican historians. Like Bancroft, the Mexican historians generally explain conditions in Mexico to a greater extent than do most American historians, and their general conclusion coincides with the Bancroft view that "pobre México" was the victim of American aggression.

7. Mexico Wanted War. Justin Harvey Smith, unlike most other American historians, went to the trouble of studying in depth conditions in Mexico prior to the Mexican War *with a view to their effects on the causes of that war.* His conclusion, unlike those of the above-mentioned schools, is that Mexico was bent on war and that the Mexican leaders refused any amicable and fair adjustment.

The major fault this author finds with most interpretations as to the causes of the Mexican War is their heavy emphasis on the United States. Interpretations such as the Slave Power Conspiracy, the Western Responsibility, Manifest Destiny, the Mercantile Theory, and Polk's Responsibility completely ignore Mexican activities and focus on those of the United States. By their very nature these interpretations imply a vacuum south of the Rio Grande.

Whether these interpretations even correctly explain

America's part is another question. Certainly, some Americans may have felt it was the manifest destiny of this nation to be a continental power. Likewise, some Westerners probably wanted more land. Also, some merchants must have desired a port on the Pacific. That any of these views predominantly explained America's role in the Mexican War, however, has not been proven by their advocates. At best, these interpretations merely reflect the motives of *some* Americans.

Regarding the Slave Power Conspiracy theory, this author finds no justification for it. This particular interpretation has been successfully rebutted by, among others, Chauncey W. Boucher. Boucher pointed out that no Southerner advocated war with Mexico for the sake of adding more slave territory prior to hostilities. Furthermore, as a reading of the *Congressional Globe* and contemporary newspapers will show, the South was hardly united on the issue of the war. John C. Calhoun, the leading Southerner of his day, was vehemently opposed to both the Mexican War and the acquisition of Mexican territory. In fact, when the Senate voted 40-2 in favor of the declaration of war, Calhoun abstained. Of the two negative votes, one—that of Senator Thomas Clayton of Delaware—came from a slave state.

Frederick Merk, in his essay on dissent during the Mexican War, pointed out that the South was hesitant about accepting the program of "All Mexico". Absorption of Mexico would have meant, the South feared, extending citizenship to colored and mixed races. This ran counter to all Southern instincts of that historical period. It clashed violently with the instincts of John C. Calhoun, the voice of Southern racism. Merk states that Calhoun's "speeches in Congress were a bitter assault on the All Mexico movement on this ground."[7]

Moreover, Calhoun felt that if any Mexican territory were to be taken, it should be only relatively unpopulated areas such as California and New Mexico. He even hesitated to accept California and New Mexico, as he doubted their suitability for

[7]Samuel Eliot Morison, Frederick Merk, and Frank Freidel, *Dissent in Three American Wars* (Cambridge: Harvard University Press, 1970), pp. 51-52.

slavery. Calhoun made it quite plain that he adamantly opposed the acquisition of any territory that might spawn free states.

Far from alone among Southerners who opposed the acquisition of Mexican territory, Calhoun was supported by Georgia Congressman Robert Toombs, who later served as Secretary of State of the Southern Confederacy. In a letter dated April 30, 1847 Toombs informed Calhoun: "You are aware of my early and uniform disrelish of the idea of the appropriation of Mexican Territory. I can see nothing but evil to come of it."[8]

In this view he was supported by David Johnson, Governor of South Carolina, who wrote to John C. Calhoun on October 26, 1847: ". . . we had done enough when we drove the Mexicans out of the territory between the Nueces and the Rio Grande; and to push the war further, for conquest and for permanent occupation, was unwise. . . ."[9]

Unfortunately for Mexico, however, its generals did not feel that enough had been done once they were put to rout across the Rio Grande by General Zachary Taylor. The Mexican generals persisted in their folly until another American general, Winfield Scott, had captured Mexico City and the Mexican army had nearly disintegrated to the point of reverting to its origin as a *bandido* gang.

Regarding President Polk's responsibility and the related American Plot theory, this book will show these theories to be false. As will be pointed out repeatedly, the Mexicans were threatening war, both before and during the Polk administration. President Polk simply reacted to Mexican threats by placing the United States in a strong defensive position. To have done otherwise would have been to neglect his duty to defend the United States. The last chapter uncovers the Mexican war plans themselves.

This leaves Justin Harvey Smith's view that Mexico wanted war as the last interpretation to be discussed. Obviously this author is more nearly in agreement with Smith than with the

[8]In Chauncey W. Boucher, "In Re That Aggressive Slaveocracy," *Mississippi Valley Historical Review*, VIII (1921), p. 36.

[9]*Ibid.*, p. 37.

other interpretations, at least as to which country bears the responsibility for causing the war.

Where this author and Smith part company, however, is over his view that Mexico actually desired war, as opposed to the belief that Mexico stumbled into a war because its military leaders refused to face reality. Smith does not, in this author's view, clearly prove that Mexico actually desired a war against the United States.

In contradistinction to Smith, this author believes that the Mexican military, by refusing to accept the reality of Texan independence, blindly pursued a course of action that could lead only to war. The Mexican military, having incited its own people to expect the subjugation of Texas, was unable to dismount the tiger of its own illusions when this prospect became totally unattainable as a result of the American annexation of Texas.

The cause of the Mexican War was the outgrowth of a purely Mexican problem: Santa Anna's overthrow of the Mexican federal constitution of 1824, which led to war with Texas and Texan independence. As the Mexican military continued to threaten Texas, the Polk administration became alarmed and took a strong defensive stance. Unable and unwilling to back down from its threats, the Mexican military was carried forward in a swift current to destruction.

In order better to understand the background of the dispute that led to the Mexican War, it is essential first to explore the colorful history of Texas and its developing ties with the United States. The first half of this book will therefore trace the growth of Texas as a distinct entity that eventually linked its destiny with that of the United States of America; the second half will deal with the direct causes of the Mexican conflict.

PART I
TEXAS

1
EARLY TEXAS

The history of modern Texas begins with Moses Austin and his son, Stephen F. Austin. The senior Austin had been a resident of Spanish Louisiana and had become a subject of the king of Spain in 1799. When in 1820 he applied to the Spanish authorities for permission to settle in Texas, Moses Austin requested the right to introduce 300 other families from Louisiana to Texas. His proposed settlement, Austin pointed out, would fulfill the intentions of King Carlos IV, expressed at the time of the Louisiana Purchase, to allow his subjects to move to any part of the Spanish dominions.

At the time of Austin's petition, Texas was an administrative division of the Viceroyalty of New Spain, known as the Eastern Interior Provinces. These provinces, in addition to Texas, included Nuevo León, Coahuila, and Nuevo Santander, later called Tamaulipas. At their head was the *comandante general,* General Joaquín de Arredondo, who exercised supreme civil and military jurisdiction in the name of Fernando VII, the King of Spain.

It was to General Arredondo that the Spanish governor of Texas, Antonio de Martínez, sent Moses Austin's petition, after having examined Austin on December 23, 1820. On the advice of the provincial deputation, a federal council representing the provinces under his jurisdiction, and in the name of the king of Spain, General Arredondo granted Austin's petition on January 17, 1821. This gave Austin the right to introduce 300 families as colonists from Louisiana into Texas. He died the following June, however, and there fell to his son, Stephen F. Austin, the task of settling colonists on the Austin grant, which covered a tract of 200,000 acres on the Colorado River. In early August, 1821, Stephen F. Austin was received by the Spanish governor of Texas, Antonio de Martínez, and recognized "without demur as heir to his father's concession."

While Stephen F. Austin was making plans for his Texan colony, a revolution had broken out in the Viceroyalty of New Spain. In the revolution the old viceroyalty fragmented, with areas such as the Philippine Islands and Cuba remaining loyal to Spain, while the rebels held the central region, which they called Mexico.

The rebel general, Agustín de Iturbide, had pronounced for independence on February 24, 1821 in what he called the "Plan de Iguala." As a result of military success and the looting of Spanish silver, Iturbide and two of his confederates, Vicente Guerrero and Guadalupe Victoria, entered Mexico City on September 27, 1821 at the head of the rebel forces. Mexican historian Alfonso Toro places the value of the Spanish silver Iturbide looted at 525,000 pesos.

Iturbide's entrance into Mexico City had been facilitated by a treaty he had made with General Juan O'Donojú in late August 1821. O'Donojú, who had been appointed Captain General of New Spain by King Fernando VII, had exceeded his authority by treating with the Mexican rebels and was shortly thereafter repudiated by his sovereign. The Treaty of Córdoba, as O'Donojú's agreement with Iturbide is known, was promptly rejected by the Spanish government when news of it reached Spain. General O'Donojú himself was disgraced and chose to remain with the rebels rather than return to Spain. The Spanish *cortes* (or Parliament), declared O'Donojú a traitor and outside the law.[1]

In spite of the illegality of the Treaty of Córdoba, the Mexicans, as they now styled themselves, considered this treaty as their recognition of independece. The Spanish government, however, did not deign to recognize the independence of Mexico until December 28, 1836 in the Treaty of Madrid.[2]

For a short period of time General Agustín de Iturbide ruled his new domain as the self-styled Emperor Agustín I. When his "empire" was overthrown by a revolution inaugurated by another adventurer, General Antonio López de Santa Anna, another fragmentation took place as the Central American provinces, Guatemala and adjacent areas, broke away.

As a result of the successful revolt against Spain, Stephen F. Austin was obliged, in 1822, to apply to the rebel authorities of revolutionized Mexico for confirmation of the concession that General Joaquín de Arredondo had granted his father on behalf of the king of Spain. A colonization law, approved by Agustín I on January 4, 1823, was promulgated, and on February 18 of that year an "Imperial Decree" confirmed Austin's Spanish grant. With the overthrow of Agustín de Iturbide, however, Stephen F. Austin was constrained to solicit still another confirmation from the current revolutionary authorities, the latter having "nullified" all of Iturbide's "imperial" decrees. On April 14, 1823 the Austin grant was confirmed by the latest set of revolutionaries.

On October 4, 1824 a congress representing the rump of the old Viceroyalty of New Spain published a federal constitution for Mexico. Lorenzo de Zavala, about whom more will be said in Chapter 3, was president of this congress. Among others, Stephen F. Austin was active in the formation of this constitution.

Under the provisions of the federal constitution of 1824, the former Spanish provinces, now called states, joined together in a federal union. In an earlier enactment, this congress had, on

[1] Alfonso Toro, *Compendio de Historia de Mexico: La Revolución de Independencia y Mexico Independiente* (Mexico City: Editorial Patria, S.A., 1958; 10th ed.), p. 265.

[2] *Ibid.*, p. 336.

January 21, 1824, passed a "Constitutive Act of the Federation," in which the old Spanish provinces were called "free, sovereign and independent states." The province of Texas, which had sparse population, was temporarily joined to the larger province of Coahuila, thus forming the state of Coahuila y Texas. The federal constitution of 1824 further provided that Texas would become a separate state from Coahuila once its population warranted such action.

The temporary union of Coahuila and Texas did not prove satisfactory to the Texans. Being the smaller entity, Texas' representation was slim, and the Coahuilans were able to dominate the dual state without difficulty. Of the 12 members of the state legislature, Texas had only one member at first, then two, and finally three. This arrangement worked to the disadvantage of the Spanish-speaking Mexican element in Texas, as well as to that of the English-speaking colonists. José Antonio Saucedo, an articulate Spanish-speaking Texan notable and friend of Stephen F. Austin, voiced the popular Texan resentment of the domination of Coahuila. In a letter to Austin dated July 14, 1826, Saucedo sarcastically stated that they were now seeing the "advantages" of the union with Coahuila.[3] In a second letter, dated July 27, 1826, Saucedo stated that Texas was losing its rights and liberty and went on to say that he had first wanted to note the conditions of union with Coahuila before agreeing to it. The *ayuntamiento* (town council) of Béxar (San Antonio) had opposed this delay, and now the results of their imprudence would be seen.[4]

Whatever the difficulties with either Coahuila or Mexico itself, Stephen F. Austin did not want Texas to break away and join the United States. Austin's creed for avoiding difficulties with Mexico was to combine loyalty and aloofness. This policy is well expressed in a letter to his brother, J. E. B. Austin, on May 10, 1823:

[3]In Eugene Campbell Barker (Ed.), *The Austin Papers* (3 vols., Washington: Government Printing Office, 1924-1928), I, part 2, p. 1371. Hereafter cited as Barker, *The Austin Papers*.

[4]*Ibid.*, p. 1390.

I wrote to the settlers on the Colorado and the Brazos that they ought not to meddle with politics, and to have nothing to do with any revolutionary schemes . . . they are as yet too recently established in the country to take an active part in its political affairs—if any questions are asked them . . . they ought to answer that they moved here to live under the government which the nation may establish . . . it is embarking on a doubtful voyage to embrace any party—as foreigners we have a good excuse for remaining neutral without being lyable [sic] to suspicions and this is the safe course.[5]

In 1822, in a letter to Josiah M. Bell and other settlers on the Colorado and Brazos Rivers, Austin stated in a similar vein:

As citizens of this, our adopted nation, it is our duty to be obedient to the laws and to unite in support of the Government, I therefore hope that the Citizens of the Colorado and Brazos will present an example of good order worthy of being followed.[6]

In another letter to his brother, J. E. B. Austin, Stephen F. Austin stated:

All our future hopes are now in this Empire [Mexico] and we must conduct ourselves so as not to loose [sic] the good name we left behind in the United States, and so as to acquire the confidence of the government we have adopted, to do this we must be correct in our deportment and rigidly faithful in all our engagements and particularly so in whatever is entrusted to us by the Government—let this be an everlasting rule for you and you will not err.[7]

From the time Spain's *comandante general,* General Joaquín de Arredondo, had granted Austin's father the original Austin grant on January 17, 1821 and Spain's Texan governor, Antonio

[5]*Ibid.*, I, part 1, p. 638.
[6]Letter of July 26, 1822, *ibid.*, p. 534.
[7]Letter of Jan. 1, 1823, *ibid.*, p. 566.

de Martínez, had recognized him as his father's heir in August, 1821, down to the decisive battle of San Jacinto on April 21, 1836, the dominant personality among the English-speaking Texans continued to be Stephen F. Austin.

Austin's policy of fidelity and gratitude toward Mexico thus became the guide for the successive waves of English-speaking colonists who arrived in Texas. In a letter to another *empresario,* Samuel M. Williams, who had settled colonists on his own grants, Austin clearly stated his policy on February 19, 1831. He informed Williams that since 1821, when he first entered Texas, he had followed a few fixed rules from which he had not deviated. Austin pointed out that he had come with pure intentions and had bid "an everlasting farewell" to his native country. In adopting Mexico he had determined to fulfill rigidly "all the duties and obligations of a *Mexican citizen.*" Austin went on to say that he had endeavored to keep all the officers with whom he "was in direct communication in a good humor, and to make friends of them."

Austin explained that he had not only excused the faults of native Mexicans, whom he referred to as his "adopted countrymen," but had even invented plausible reasons to justify or explain away all their political errors. Regarding the Mexicans, Austin stated:

> I have been silent as to all their defects, and lavish of praise where there was the least pretext for bestowing it, but at the same time decissive [sic] and unbending where a constitutional or vested right of vital importance was directly attacked. Rights of minor consideration I have paid no attention to, for bad feeling might be engendered about *trifles,* that would jeapordise [sic] an important interest. To sum up all I have endeavored to do my duty as a *Mexican citizen.*[8]

Exactly one year later, on February 19, 1832, in a letter to his sister, Mrs. Mary Austin Holley, Austin again expressed his loyalty to Mexico. Emphasizing the importance of never even giving the appearance of disloyalty, he wrote:

[8]Letter of Feb. 19, 1831, *ibid.,* II, pp. 600-601.

How cautious ought we to be, in all stations of life, but especially in places where our opinions and expressions are liable to be misunderstood or perverted for evil purposes, never to deviate, even *in appearance* from permanent rules of action. You know that my motto is *fidelity to Mexico*. I never departed from it, and never intend to depart from it.[9]

The Mexicans, however, did not appreciate the loyalty and fidelity of Stephen F. Austin and the Texans. Apparently, also, the Mexicans chose to forget that the Texan colonists were invited by Spain, in the first place, to serve as a bulwark against warring Indians. The Texans were originally seen as the buffer between the Indians of the North and those colonists living further south in the rest of the Eastern Interior Provinces of the Viceroyalty of New Spain.

On the subject of Texas as a buffer zone against the Indians, Austin wrote on January 14, 1834:

Without population in Texas the frontiers of the Eastern Interior Provinces are worse than nothing, for they are an abandoned field where the Indians may rob, kill, and destroy to suit their fancy, without protection for the wretched people. It would be an enormous expense to maintain garrisons and troops enough to restrain the Indian even in a small degree in deserts so vast.[10]

Instead of aiding the growth of population in Texas by encouraging its economic prosperity, the officials in Mexico City constantly thwarted Austin's commercial endeavors.

Austin had hoped to develop a coastwise trade between the Texans and the Mexicans, which would thus establish commercial ties and cement the union by common interest and personal friendship. He was also interested in the planting of various crops. On these subjects Austin was in communication with most of the important men of Mexico. His letter of September 20, 1828 to General Manuel de Mier y Terán is a treatise in favor of

[9]*Ibid.*, p. 753.
[10]Austin to Rafael Llanos, Jan. 14, 1834, *ibid.*, p. 1029.

29

cotton as a plant well suited to Texas. It is also a plea for the establishment of a coastwise trade between Texas and Mexico.[11]

Mexican reaction to the growth of Texas was, however, negative. In September 1829 General Mier y Terán became Mexican *comandante general* of the Eastern Interior States (formerly known as the Eastern Interior Provinces under Spain, and referred to as such by Austin in his letter of January 14, 1834) and therefore responsible for the defense of Texas. His recommendations to the government of General Anastasio Bustamante, then serving as President in Mexico City, led to the Law of April 6, 1830. The intent of this law was to stop the flow of immigration into Texas from the United States.

General Mier y Terán's major proposals were to establish a military occupation of Texas, to countercolonize Texas with Mexicans and Europeans, as opposed to Americans, and to develop an economic bond between Texas and the rest of Mexico. In this latter idea, Stephen F. Austin's influence is rather apparent. The general's desire to fill Texas with non-Americans was based on a fear and dislike of the United States. In a letter to the Mexican Foreign Minister, Lucas Alamán, on January 14, 1830, General Mier y Terán's aide, Colonel Constantino Tarnava, suggested that England be induced to make a declaration against American "designs" on Texas. Colonel Tarnava also suggested on two separate occasions in his long letter that Mexican convicts be sent to help populate Texas. In his concluding sentence Colonel Tarnava advised Foreign Minister Alamán to appoint a Mexican consular agent at New Orleans to spy on the United States. Tarnava referred to the Americans as "our neighbors, who are almost now our enemies."[12]

It is interesting to note that the Tarnava letter was written in 1830, some 16 years before the outbreak of the Mexican War, yet is obviously very hostile to the United States.

The Mexicans did attempt to foist a criminal population upon Texas, but on the whole were not successful. Mexican

[11]*Ibid.*, pp. 116-118.

[12]University of Texas Transcripts (from the Department of Fomento, Mexico, legajo 5, expediente 30), Barker History Center, Austin, Texas.

convicts did not want to move hundreds of miles away to a hot underpopulated land, where it would be nigh impossible to steal for a living and where they must actually work for their daily bread each day, not *mañana*. The small "success" that Mexico did achieve in sending criminals to Texas was mainly in regard to their convict-soldiers, which Texans frequently mentioned as a grievance against Mexico. In Chapter 4 it will be pointed out that one of the stipulations made by the victorious Texans after General Edward Burleson defeated Santa Anna's brother-in-law, General Martín Perfecto de Cós, on December 11, 1835 was that General Cós take his convict-soldiers beyond the Rio Grande. This stipulation formed one of the articles of capitulation the defeated General Cós was compelled to sign.

The recruitment of European immigrants to Texas proved too costly, as General Mier y Terán himself admitted, and was abandoned.[13] However, Mier y Terán did achieve at least one of his objectives, that of scattering garrisons at strategic points amongst the Texan population, and thus obtained as much of a military occupation as was possible, given the vast distances and the sparse population.

[13]Manuel de Mier y Terán to Stephen F. Austin., March 21, 1831, in Barker, *The Austin Papers*, II, p. 622.

2
Coahuila y Texas

Moves designed to gain Texas' separation from the state of Coahuila, while still remaining within the Mexican federation, were undertaken in 1832 and 1833. As will be seen, Stephen F. Austin represented the more moderate element in this separatist movement, one that did not seek independence from Mexico, but rather greater autonomy for Texas.

In 1832, in response to a call from the *ayuntamiento* (town council) of San Felipe, a number of Texan delegates assembled in convention, which adopted a petition favoring the separation of Texas from Coahuila. Before the convention adjourned, it created committees of correspondence and a standing central committee. It also delegated William H. Wharton to go to Mexico City to present its opinions.

Unfortunately, while the Mexican population of San Antonio de Béxar agreed that the reforms suggested by the convention were justified, they declined to participate. The Mexican-Texans explained that the convention was ill-timed because a revolution, headed by Mexico's perennial adventurer, General Antonio López de Santa Anna, was then in progress. The Texans, who had been having their difficulties with the régime of General Anastasio Bustamante and its agents, such as General Manuel de Mier y Terán, had seized the opportunity to announce their support for the Santa Anna uprising. But the Mexican-Texans pointed out that by declaring for Santa Anna, who could do nothing for them as he was not yet in power, the Texans had cut themselves off from whatever favorable action they might have otherwise expected from President Bustamante. Once order was restored, however, the Mexican-Texans clearly stated, they would be willing to cooperate with the Texans in lawful ways.

Ramón Músquiz, the political chief of San Antonio de Béxar, echoed these sentiments. In a letter to Austin, Músquiz, who represented the largest single concentration of Mexicans in Texas, stated that the *ayuntamiento* of San Felipe, where the English-speaking Texans predominated, had acted illegally in calling for the convention. Nevertheless, Músquiz went on, he was not opposed to the objectives the *ayuntamiento* of San Felipe had in mind and wished to further them to the limit of his legal power.[1]

Stephen F. Austin, who preferred to have the Mexican population of Texas take the lead in the movement for reform, attempted to gain the support of the Mexican-Texans for a separate state of Texas within the Mexican federation. The central committee set up by the 1832 convention, however, called a convention in 1833. This 1833 convention was in session from April 1 to April 13. Its major accomplishment was a petition against the union with Coahuila, which it pointed out was intended by the Mexican federal constitution of 1824 to be temporary. The convention then nominated Stephen F. Austin to carry the petition to Mexico City.

While the more radical Texans were thus striving for a separate statehood for Texas within the Mexican federation, but apart from Coahuila, Stephen F. Austin was attempting to achieve the same ends through more regular channels. Lucas Alamán, author of a classic history of Mexico, a cabinet minister, and a leading member of the Bustamante régime, told Austin, in

[1]Letter of Oct. 11, 1832 in Barker, *The Austin Papers*, II, p. 875.

a letter dated April 6, 1831, that he was persuaded that separation was in the best interests of both Texas and Coahuila.[2] This was in response to two letters Austin had written to Alamán on the subject of separating the two states.

While he favored separation from Coahuila, Austin by no means desired independence for Texas, nor did he desire that Texas become a part of the United States. Austin was still a loyal Mexican citizen. In a letter to Ramón Músquiz, the political chief of San Antonio de Béxar, dated March 29, 1830, Austin adamantly opposed the idea that Mexico should sell Texas to the United States. Austin made it plain that he spoke for the general population, and he voiced the strong objection of the Texans against the reported rumors that Mexico intended to sell Texas. The fears that Mexico would sell Texas never materialized, and the United States chargé d'affaires, Anthony Butler, who was suspected of intriguing to purchase Texas, was later recalled by President Andrew Jackson.

On behalf of the Texans, Austin stated, however:

> We believe in the first place that the national government [of Mexico] does not have any constitutional authority to sell or dismember any part of a state of the federation without the prior consent of the state which it is attempting to dismember, and also without the special consent of the people which it is attempting to sell. We do not believe that the people of Texas are cattle to be sold at the will of the national government.
>
> We believe that the right to dispose of the public lands of the state of Coahuila y Texas belongs solely and exclusively to the state and not to the nation.
>
> We believe that Texas should have the right to form a state of this federation [of Mexico] since it has the necessary elements, and therefore the right to dispose of the public lands of Texas that belong to the state of Texas.
>
> We believe that it is not fitting in any way to pass to the government of the North [the United States] without a prior guarantee plainly recognizing the right which the inhabitants of Texas have to form their own constitution without any restric-

[2]*Ibid.*, pp. 641-642.

tion, and recognizing particularly the right that the people of Texas have to dispose of their public lands and negating in the absolute any right on the part of the national government of involving itself in any way with the public lands of Texas, or with the concessions of lands already made to particular persons either under the Spanish government or under this [Mexican] government. We believe that if Mexico sells us without our consent, it would be better to declare ourselves independent of the entire world, before passing to another power without prior guarantees recognizing all the constitutional rights of the people of Texas.[3]

The above section forms part of a much longer letter that reiterates the points already covered. This letter, which was written in Spanish and is thus additional proof that Austin took his loyalty to Mexico seriously, furthermore serves as evidence that Austin and the Texans did not see themselves as agents of the United States who had been planted in Texas in order ultimately to extend American sovereignty over that piece of real estate. Austin's loyalty to Mexico and his desire that Texas not become a part of the United States appear constantly in his correspondence.

In a letter to General Manuel de Mier y Terán, dated September 17, 1830, Austin states:

I don't want to see Texas separated from Mexico, but if it ever becomes necessary, in order to save it from complete ruin, I believe it would be better to declare ourselves independent of the world, before uniting ourselves to the north [the United States].[4]

In a letter to Mrs. Mary Austin Holley, his sister, dated December 29, 1831 Austin expresses himself strongly against joining the United States:

One word from me *now* would anihilate [sic] every Mexican soldier in Texas. But I am opposed to all violence—all

[3]Austin to Ramón Músquiz, Mar. 29, 1830, *ibid.*, pp. 354-355.
[4]*Ibid.*, p. 486.

36

bloodshed—so long as there is even a plausible hope of avoiding such extremes. And I am opposed to a separation from Mexico, if the government will treat us as we merit, and as the true interests of the Country require.

Our situation is extremely delicate and interesting. To remain as we are, is impossible. We have not the right kind of material for an Independent Government, and a union with the United States would bring Negro Slavery—that curse of curses, and worst of reproaches, on civilized man; that unanswered, and unanswerable, inconsistency of *free* and liberal republicans. I think the Government will yield, and give us what we ought to have [statehood for Texas within the Mexican federation, but separate from Coahuila]. If not, we shall go for *Independence*, and put our trust in our selves, our riffles [sic], and—our God.[5]

Reading Austin's correspondence with Mexican officials, friends, and relatives makes the reasons for the fierce opposition to union with the United States on the part of many Texans apparent. Stephen F. Austin and other Texas landowners were concerned lest their territorial concessions not be accepted by the United States. Furthermore, many Texans, like the Virginia-born Austin, were opposed to slavery and feared that, if Texas were annexed to the United States, it would be drawn into the orbit of America's slaveocracy.

In spite of his abhorrence of slavery, Austin had none the less lobbied in Mexico City for a contract labor law permitting the continued introduction of slaves into Texas as indentured servants. This had been necessary, Austin felt, in order to populate the Province. However, to join the United States, Austin feared, would make permanent the institution of slavery, which he had hoped would be a transitory phenomenon in the history of Texas.

In early 1833 Austin left Texas for Mexico City. His mission was to obtain separate statehood for Texas within the Mexican federation. He reached Mexico City on July 18. On August 1 he filed an argument with Carlos García, the Mexican minister of foreign relations, which supported the right of Texas to statehood within the Mexican federation. Austin based his argument

[5]*Ibid.*, p. 730.

on six basic points. First, Texas possessed sufficient qualifications for statehood, and the Texans desired it. Second, Texas had been a separate Spanish province before the establishment of the Mexican federation, and like any other original member of the federation, had the right to separate statehood. Third, the provisional union of Texas with Coahuila, by the Mexican law of May 7, 1824, guaranteed Texas the right of establishing herself as a state when, in the opinion of the inhabitants of Texas, she possessed the necessary elements for statehood. Fourth, the right to statehood was guaranteed to Texas by the federal system, which Mexico adopted, of promoting her welfare and securing her prosperity and tranquility by an adequate organization of local autonomy. Fifth, it was the duty of the Texan people to remove every obstacle that interfered with cementing their loyalty to Mexico, and the union with Coahuila was such an obstacle. Sixth, Austin finally appealed to the natural right that all people have of saving themselves from anarchy and ruin.

Austin went on to explain his six basic points in detail. Concerning the provisional union of Texas and Coahuila by the Mexican law of May 7, 1824, he stated that it "was without the formal or cordial consent of the people of Texas, or of her deputy in the general constituent congress." Austin continued that the natural right of Texas to statehood was recognized by the law of May 7, 1824, "by the fact that the union with Coahuila is *conditional* and *provisional,* and not *positive* and *permanent.*" Austin closed this segment of his argument by stating that the provisions in the Mexican constitution that called for three-fourths of the states in the Mexican federation to approve the admission of new states did not apply to Texas, which had always had the right to be a separate state.

In his lengthy argument Austin scored certain other points. He stated quite candidly "*that Coahuila cannot govern Texas and the latter cannot remain, and will not remain in harmony or quietude with the former.*" Again Austin stated that it was in the best interests of Texas "*to cement her union with Mexico, and to have a local government as a state of this federation.*"

In a final sally Austin stated that, without separate statehood, Texas would be reduced to anarchy. Austin then said:

A state of anarchy in Texas would also cause confusion upon the frontiers of Louisiana and Arkansas; and in such case the probability is great that the government of the north [United States] would take possession of Texas in order to preserve order upon their frontiers as it did in the case of the Floridas.

All this and incalculable other evils would be avoided by establishing Texas as a state.[6]

In September 1833 the Mexican congress resumed its sessions, but failed to act on the Texas question. Austin, now desperate, informed Valentín Gómez Farías, the acting president in the absence of Santa Anna, that the Texans would not submit to further delay.

Austin next wrote to the *ayuntamiento* of San Antonio de Béxar. In his letter Austin recommended that the *ayuntamientos* of Texas place themselves in immediate communication with each other for the purpose of organizing a state government for Texas within the Mexican federation, based on the guarantee of the law of May 7, 1824. Austin had despaired of getting the Mexican congress to approve statehood for Texas, and he wished to present Mexico with a *fait accompli*.

This letter of October 2, 1833 proved most unfortunate for Austin. First of all, the *ayuntamiento* of San Antonio de Béxar declined to take the lead in forming a state government. Instead, it sent a copy of the letter to the governor of Coahuila y Texas, who forwarded it to Acting President Valentín Gómez Farías. The latter reacted to Austin's letter by having him arrested on January 3, 1834 when Austin, who was returning to Texas, innocently walked into the office of the *comandante general* in Saltillo.

In spite of his arrest, Austin remained a Mexican patriot. On January 12, 1834 he wrote to his fellow *empresario*, Samuel M. Williams:

> I hope there will be no excitement about my arrest. All I can be accused of is, that I have labored arduously, faithfully, and perhaps at particular moments, pationately [sic], and with more impatience and irritation than I ought to have shewn [sic], to

[6]Austin to Carlos García, Aug. 1, 1833, *ibid.*, pp. 992-996.

have Texas made a State of the Mexican Confederation separate from Coahuila. This is all, and this is no crime.[7]

This message was constantly repeated in Austin's letters. In writing to his brother-in-law, James F. Perry, on January 16 Austin said:

> All the people have to do is to remain quiet and let Bexar [where the Mexican element predominated] take the lead in everything.
>
> I hope there will be no excitement on account of my arrest, it will do me harm and great harm to Texas—keep quiet and let me perish if such is to be my fate. . . .
>
> My advice to Texas is, what it has always been [;] remain quiet—populate the country—improve your farms—and discountenance all kind of revolutionary men or principles. If this advice is followed that country will prosper. So long as you belong to Coahuila, obey the laws and the authorities of that State.[8]

Austin was determined that the Texans should not rebel against Mexico. In addition to his private letters to friends and relatives, Austin also wrote to the *ayuntamiento* of San Felipe, the main settlement of the English-speaking Texan colonists. His advice was to keep the peace:

> I do not in any manner blame the government for arresting me, and I particularly request that there may be no excitement about it.
>
> I give the advice to the people there that I have always given, keep quiet, discountenance all revolutionary measures or men, obey the state authorities and laws so long as you are attached to Coahuila, have no more conventions, petition through the legal channels, that is through the ayuntamiento and chief of department, harmonize fully with the people of Bexar and Goliad, and act with them.[9]

Ultimately, as part of a general amnesty, Austin was released on June 22, 1835, and he returned to Texas.

[7]*Ibid.*, pp. 1024-1025.
[8]*Ibid.*, p. 1038.
[9]Letter of Jan. 17, 1834, *ibid.*, p. 1039.

3
Mexican Federalistas

While Stephen F. Austin was having his personal problems with the Mexicans, a feud developed in the state of Coahuila y Texas amongst the Mexicans themselves. The conflict originated in the removal of the state capital from Saltillo to Monclova, by a decree of the state legislature on March 9, 1833.

To complicate matters further, in May 1834 reactionary elements of the Mexican army and clergy drew up the Plan of Cuernavaca, in which they denounced all liberal reforms, and called upon President Antonio López de Santa Anna to dissolve congress and rule as a dictator. Santa Anna only too gladly acceded to these demands. He not only dissolved congress, but ruled without a council of government and even without ministers. Next, Santa Anna disbanded the state legislatures and deposed governors. Finally he buried the ten-year-old Mexican federal constitution of 1824. These activities led to revolts in some of the states, such as Zacatecas, Yucatán, and Coahuila y Texas, by supporters of the federal constitution of 1824, who were called *federalistas*.

In Coahuila y Texas, the executive council and the perma-

41

nent deputation of the legislature on June 24, 1834 jointly issued a protest against the Santa Anna-supported Plan of Cuernavaca. Furthermore, it called a special meeting of the state legislature, then not in session, to take steps for the "safety of the confederation [and] for the permanent restoration of the public tranquility, at present interrupted by collisions of the supreme national authorities."[1]

Seeing a chance to recoup its former position as capital of Coahuila y Texas, the city of Saltillo on July 19, 1834 pronounced for Santa Anna and the Plan of Cuernavaca. The governor of Coahuila y Texas, Agustín de Viesca in Monclova, was repudiated; a rival Saltillo governor was set up; and all laws passed by the state legislature since its removal to Monclova were declared void.

In spite of Saltillo's support, Santa Anna declared that Monclova was the rightful capital of Coahuila y Texas. The city of Saltillo, however, refused to accept Santa Anna's decision. In this Saltillo was encouraged by the *comandante general* of the Eastern Interior States, General Martín Perfecto de Cós, brother-in-law of Santa Anna. On March 12, 1835 the Saltillo deputies withdrew from the legislature.

On March 14, 1835 the state legislature of Coahuila y Texas passed a law authorizing Governor Viesca to sell 400 leagues of public land. General Cós, who now had a pretext, declared this law contrary to the federal colonization law and ordered his troops to invade Coahuila y Texas and occupy the state capital of Monclova. In response, the state legislature of Coahuila y Texas on April 7, 1835 authorized Governor Viesca to call up the state militia for defense.

It should be emphasized that the Texan colonists, up to this point, had held themselves aloof from the squabbles among the Mexicans. The Texans did not like the land sales the state legislature had authorized, and consequently they did not respond to Governor Agustín de Viesca's call for a militia to defend

---

[1]Hans Peter Nielson Gammel [Compiler], *The Laws of Texas: 1822-1897*, (2 vols., Austin: The Gammel Book Co., 1898), I, p. 388. Hereafter cited as Gammel, *Laws of Texas*.

Coahuila y Texas against the invasion of the *comandante general,* General Martín Perfecto de Cós.

The Texans had apparently misunderstood the situation. It will be remembered that the state government of Coahuila y Texas had denounced Santa Anna's assumption of dictatorial powers and the reactionary Plan of Cuernavaca. General Martín Perfecto de Cós, furthermore, was merely a satrap of his brother-in-law, dictator Santa Anna. By invading the state of Coahuila y Texas with *santannista* troops, General Cós hoped to forestall the type of insurrection then raging in the state of Zacatecas. The Zacatecans were fighting against the Santa Anna dictatorship and in favor of the Mexican federal constitution of 1824. Before the legislature of Coahuila y Texas adjourned on May 21, 1835, it authorized Governor Viesca at his discretion to move the seat of government, to prevent it from falling into the hands of the *santannista* soldiers under General Cós. Governor Viesca did attempt to move the state government to San Antonio de Béxar, in Texas, but he was captured by the *santannistas* before he could do so.

On January 28, 1835 Santa Anna's new puppet congress had removed Vice President Valentín Gómez Farías from office. On March 31 Santa Anna had congress pass a law reducing the state militias to one man per every 500 inhabitants. This reduction would have had the effect of weakening the power of the states to resist the new *santannista* dictatorship. General Santa Anna in the meantime placed himself at the head of the army and marched into the state of Zacatecas to force the acceptance of the Plan of Cuernavaca and the destruction of the Mexican federal constitution of 1824. After a bloodbath, Santa Anna was successful.

On May 2, 1835 the *santannista* congress declared that it possessed "extra-constitutional powers" to make such changes in the Mexican federal constitution of 1824 as it thought best without subjecting itself to the regular constitutional process prescribed in the constitution.

Dictator Santa Anna's first step in exerting his authority over Coahuila y Texas had been the appointment of his brother-in-law, General Cós, as *comandante general* of the Eastern Interior

States. General Cós, in turn, appointed Colonel Domingo de Ugartechea as the *comandante* of Texas.

Meanwhile, back in January, 1835, Captain Antonio Tenorio, a *santannista* officer under the command of Colonel Ugartechea, had arrived at the Texan port of Anahuac with a detachment of soldiers to reopen the customs house. Some of the Texan merchants there, most notable among whom was Andrew Briscoe, objected to the enforcement of the tariff as they felt it was not being enforced in other Texan ports. As a result of mutual irritation and practical jokes played on the *santannista* troops, Andrew Briscoe and a friend were arrested.

News of the Briscoe affair reached San Felipe in June of 1835 through a military courier. The latter delivered a letter from General Cós to James B. Miller, the political chief of San Felipe. The letter told of the suspension of civil government in Monclova and of the arrest of Governor Viesca. In spite of the fact that the Texan colonists had disliked the land sales legislation of the Viesca régime at Monclova and had refused to obey Governor Viesca's call for militia, they were now aroused. A group of Texans gathered around the courier and seized other letters he was carrying. Among the letters seized was one from General Cós to Captain Tenorio, assuring the latter that heavy reinforcements were on the way. Another letter, from Colonel Ugartechea, assured Tenorio that the *santannista* troops that had crushed Zacatecas were then at Saltillo, en route to Texas.

As a result of the mail seizures and the disclosure of the contemplated military action of the *santannista* officers, the Texans called a meeting. James B. Miller presided, and later issued a proclamation calling upon the men of San Felipe to march to Governor Viesca's rescue and bring him to Texas in order to reestablish the state govermment of Coahuila y Texas.

On the following day Robert M. Williamson, one of the Texan settlers, presided over a second meeting. Resolutions were adopted reviewing Santa Anna's violations of both the Mexican federal constitution of 1824 and the state constitution of Coahuila y Texas. The resolutions further declared that it was the intention of the Texans to maintain the two constitutions in their original republican character. A few days later, in a Fourth of July address, Williamson gave the additional information that the meeting resolved to capture San Antonio de Béxar, take possession of the military equipment collected there, and install the vice-governor, Ramón Músquiz, at the head of a provisional government pending the release of Governor Agustín de Viesca.

While the Texan town of San Felipe was thus preparing to meet the *santannista* invasion and to fight to retain the Mexican federal constitution of 1824, which Santa Anna had been demolishing, there was action in the port of Anahuac. The noted William Travis, later to die at the Alamo, was enlisting volunteers to expel Captain Tenorio, which he successfully did on June 30, 1835.

When Travis returned to San Felipe, however, the public mood had changed. Both his own action at Anahuac and the San Felipe meeting of June 22 came under attack. A meeting at Columbia, Texas on June 28, 1835 condemned those actions calculated to involve the Texans in a conflict with the "federal" government of Mexico. The Columbia meeting, furthermore, declared that separation from Mexico was neither the wish nor in the interest of the people. At the same time it exhorted the Texans to adhere strictly to the constitution of 1824 and the law and urged the political chief to take steps to defend the frontier from Indian depredations.

It is obvious, of course, that a militia organized to fight Indians could easily be turned against *santannistas*. Also, since Santa Anna had overthrown the Mexican federal constitution of 1824, adherence to that document set the Texans against the dictator. The tone of the Columbia meeting, however, was pacific, and there is no indication that the Texans wanted war. As other Texan communities followed Columbia's lead, both Political Chief James B. Miller of San Felipe and William Travis were put on the defensive. Without further provocation from the *santannistas*, the Texans would remain at peace.

This, however, was not to be. General Martín Perfecto de Cós issued a requisition for the arrest of a number of Texans, including William Travis. Colonel Domingo de Ugartechea was ordered to enforce the requisition. In addition, General Cós refused to receive a peace commission until Travis and the others were handed over. With large reinforcements arriving, it was becoming ever more obvious that General Cós intended to establish military rule in Texas.

The Texan response to the *santannista* invasion of General Cós was to call a consultation, to meet on October 15, 1835 at Washington-on-the-Brazos.

It should be remembered at this point that Stephen F. Austin, who had been a Mexican prisoner since January 3, 1834, was released on June 22, 1835. When Austin reappeared in Texas, he was treated as a returning hero, and dinners were given in his honor. All Texas waited to hear how Austin would respond to the invasion of General Cós. Austin's power and influence over the Texan settlers were unequaled. As long as Austin urged restraint, Texas held back. Austin was for many years Texas incarnate.

On September 8, 1835, at a public dinner in Brazoria, Texas given in his honor, Austin for the first time urged resistance. He stated that there was a revolution in Mexico, the object of which was to change the form of government by destroying the federal constitution of 1824 and establishing a central or consolidated government. The states would be converted into provinces. He further stated:

> Under the Spanish government, Texas was a separate and distinct local organization. It was one of the unities that composed the general mass of the nation . . . and was represented in the constituent congress of Mexico, that formed the constitution of 1824. This constituent congress, so far from destroying this unity, expressly recognized and confirmed it by the law of May 7, 1824, which united Texas with Coahuila *provisionally*, under the especial guarantee of being made a state of the Mexican confederation, as soon as it possessed the necessary elements. That law and the federal constitution gave to Texas a specific political existence, and vested in its inhabitants special and defined rights, which can only be relinquished by the people of Texas, acting for themselves as a unity, and not as a part of

Coahuila, for the reason that the union with Coahuila, was *limited,* and only gave power to the state of Coahuila and Texas to govern Texas for the time being, but *always subject to the vested rights of Texas.* The state, therefore, cannot relinquish those vested rights, by agreeing to the change of government, or by any other act, unless expressly authorized by the people of Texas to do so; neither can the general government of Mexico legally deprive Texas of them without the consent of this people. These are my opinions.[2]

Austin went on to say that he had no doubt that the federal constitution of 1824 would be destroyed. What was now needed, Austin stated, was a "general consultation of the people by means of delegates elected for that purpose, with full powers . . . to adopt such measures as the tranquility and salvation of the country may require."[3]

Stephen F. Austin had now called for a general consultation of the people of Texas. This was Austin's answer to Martin Perfecto de Cós and the *santannista* invasion of Texas. This consultation, as previously mentioned, was scheduled to meet on October 15, 1835 at Washington-on-the-Brazos.

At this point it would be inappropriate to continue without mentioning Lorenzo de Zavala. Of all the Mexicans involved in the later independence of Texas, the role of Lorenzo de Zavala is the most prominent. Zavala resigned as Mexican minister to France early in 1835 and departed from France for the United States. Upon arriving in New York in May, 1835, he made known to the Mexican government his intentions of settling in Texas.[4] Zavala cited as his reasons his desire to live apart from the struggle of factional politics in Mexico City and his wish to rebuild his personal fortune, which had deteriorated during his long political career.

Evidence exists, however, that Lorenzo de Zavala hoped to

[2] Austin's address at Brazoria on the neccessity of a consultation, in Barker, *The Austin Papers,* III, pp. 117-118.

[3] *Ibid.,* p. 118.

[4] Lorenzo de Zavala to J. Moreno, May 8, 1835, in Carlos García Papers, University of Texas Archives, Latin American collection, Austin, Texas.

incite a revolution in Texas, place himself at the head, and go on to defeat Santa Anna and abolish the centralist régime. Evidence also exists that Zavala had secretly advocated the formation of a northern Mexican republic modeled on that of the United States. The idea of promoting a Texan revolution was something that Zavala had considered as far back as 1830.[5]

On July 3, 1835 Zavala arrived in New Orleans en route to Texas. He remained in New Orleans only four days before continuing on to Texas. As New Orleans served as an entrepôt for Texas, however, both as regards people and products, Zavala could observe the political sympathies of several prominent individuals regarding the situation prevailing in Texas at that time. Raymond Estep, in his biography of Zavala, suggests that Zavala probably discussed his Texas plans with many Mexican liberals (*federalistas*) who had been exiled by the centralist (*santannista*) régime in Mexico and had found refuge in New Orleans.[6]

At any rate, Zavala took advantage of the first opportunity to leave for Texas and set sail on the *San Felipe* on July 7, 1835, arriving at Brazoria, Texas about July 10. Zavala quickly joined the more radical Texans, approving their plans. His speedy involvement with the Texan radicals serves as further proof that he had set a course of action for himself, prior to his arrival, that was to encourage a revolt against the *santannista* government in Mexico City. Estep points out:

> So anxious was he [Lorenzo de Zavala] to take part in the plans of the insurgent leaders, that toward the fifteenth of July—within

[5]New Orleans *Union* (editorial), Nov. 23, 1835; Joaquín M. Castillo y Lanzas to the Secretario de Estado y del Despacho de Relaciones Exteriores, Feb. 17, 1836, in the Mexican Archives (Archivo General de la Secretaría de Relaciones Exteriores, México, Asuntos Internacionales, Estados Unidos, 1835-1836, transcriptions), University of Texas Archives, Barker History Center, Austin, Texas; *Washington Globe*, June 28, 1836; New Orleans *Bee*, June 11, 1836; Anthony Butler to Andrew Jackson, May 25, 1831, in William Ray Manning (Ed.), *Diplomatic Correspondence of the United States: Inter-American Affairs*, vol. VIII, 1831-1860 (Washington: Carnegie Endowment for International Peace, 1937), p. 244, hereafter cited as Manning, *Diplomatic History of the United States*, VIII; United States Congress, House, 25th Congress, 2nd session, Executive Document No. 351, XII, p. 382.

[6]Raymond Estep, *Lorenzo de Zavala: Profeta del Liberalismo Mexicano* (Mexico City: Librería de Manuel Porrua, 1952), p. 290. Hereafter cited as Estep, *Lorenzo de Zavala*.

five days following his arrival in Brazoria—he was already trying to discover the attitude of the people toward a revolution.[7]

In spite of Lorenzo de Zavala's enthusiasm for a revolution, he received a frosty reception in Columbia, whose English speaking residents were suspicious that a Mexican wished to lead them in a revolt.

Zavala's fast pace of activities was now causing increased concern to the *santannista* officials, both in Mexico City and in Texas. His immediate arrest and extradition to Mexico City were soon ordered by the government of General Antonio López de Santa Anna. Zavala, however, was well protected by his new Texan friends and quite at liberty to promote a revolution.

During the summer of 1835 Zavala visited most of the leaders of the more radical Texans. Also, the Texan colonists who had originally received Zavala's insinuations of revolt so coldly in Columbia were finally impressed by his revolutionary zeal and enthusiasm. He was requested to speak at a patriotic meeting at Lynch's Ferry on August 8, 1835. This was Zavala's great opportunity, and he immediately accepted.

Unfortunately, however, Zavala became bedridden with an intermittent fever and was forced to send a written address. In this communication, Zavala analyzed the political situation of Mexico and denounced Santa Anna as a traitor to federalism. Furthermore, Zavala contended, Santa Anna had lost all right to the loyalty of the Mexican people. Next, Zavala proposed that a convention be called for the purpose of dealing in detail with the problems of Texas and the need of cooperation among the *federalistas*. In his address, which was delivered one month before Austin spoke at Brazoria calling for a consultation, Zavala suggested that October 15 be the date when the convention he had proposed should meet. The idea of a general meeting did not take hold until Austin's Brazoria address, and it was Austin's term "consultation" that prevailed. None the less, it was Zavala who first suggested the idea of a meeting and the October 15 date, which was the time the consultation was scheduled to meet.

[7]*Ibid.*, p. 291.

While Lorenzo de Zavala was trying to convince the Texans to revolt against the Santa Anna dictatorship, other Mexican *federalistas*, refugees from the dictator and based in New Orleans, were inaugurating a few steps of their own. These Mexican exiles set up a *junta* and called a meeting for September 4, 1835 in New Orleans. Under the auspices of this *junta* a plan was set in motion to overthrow Santa Anna and re-establish federalism.

Furthermore, the *junta* designated former Vice President Valentín Gómez Farías, who had also served as President *ad interim* of Mexico before being deposed by Santa Anna; Colonel José Antonio Mexía (Mejía), and Lorenzo de Zavala, who did not attend the New Orleans meeting, as he preferred to remain in Texas, as chiefs of the movement to restore federalism in Mexico. Valentín Gómez Farías was named to head an executive committee based in New Orleans; Colonel José Antonio Mexía was designated commander-in-chief of the *federalista* army of liberation; and Lorenzo de Zavala was named director of the Texan colonists. Zavala's task was to obtain arms, money, and soldiers from the Texans. While Zavala was thus to concentrate on Texas, Colonel Mexía was to occupy the Mexican port of Tampico.[8]

The exiled Mexican *junta* further resolved that the anti-liberal members of the Mexican clergy should themselves be exiled and that church property should be confiscated. The *federalista* exiles next planned an alliance between the United States and a post-Santa Anna Mexico. This alliance was to be aimed against England, whose subjects were to be prohibited from entering Mexican territory in large numbers. Finally, the influence of the British government on Mexico was to be eliminated.[9]

Zavala in the meantime had purchased a home in Buffalo Bayou, Texas and continued his intimate cooperation with the

[8]Joaquín M. Castillo y Lanzas to the Secretario del Despacho de Relaciones Exteriores, Feb. 17, 1836, in the Mexican Archives (Archivo General de la Secretaría de Relaciones Exteriores, Mexico, Asuntos Internacionales, Estados Unidos, 1835-1836, transcripts), University of Texas Archives, Barker History Center, Austin, Texas.

[9]*El Mosquito Mexicano*, Mexico City, Dec. 11, 1835.

leaders of the incipient Texas rebellion.[10] In this autumn of 1835 it seems that only Stephen F. Austin and Lorenzo de Zavala understood the relative strength of Texas and the relative weakness of Mexico. The strength of Texas lay in its geographical continuity of settlements and the basic unity of its people against the Santa Anna dictatorship. Mexico, while larger in area and population, was divided geographically by mountains and deserts, by different Indian tribes that varied in their degree of hispanization, and by the general Latin American lack of unity and malaise of constantly competing political factions, with their own military chieftains plotting the next coup d'état.

Writing to Austin on September 17, 1835, Zavala pointed out that there were two points of view in existence in Texas. The minority advocated absolute independence. The majority, Zavala stated, was wasting its time in useless discussion. At this juncture Zavala considered both groups dangerous.

Zavala, who was hoping to elevate himself to power in Mexico by means of a Texas revolution that was to be part of the *federalista* movement, took up the subject of Texan independence with Austin. Zavala felt that complete separation of Texas from Mexico at this time was inopportune. None the less, recognizing the incompatibility of the military régime that governed Mexico with the "rights, customs, education, and principles of the Texan people," the latter ought to establish an ordinance of provisional independence from the Mexican government. In such a condition of provisional independence, Zavala felt Texas should maintain the rights assured her according to the social contract and later to join in a federation with the other Mexican states, which he hoped would recover their lost rights within a period of two years.[11]

Zavala was completely opposed to Austin's suggestion of September 15, 1835 to defend the federal constitution of 1824 in its entirety. Zavala, while a staunch *federalista* and supporter of

[10]William P. Harris and John W. Moore to Stephen F. Austin, Sept. 23, 1835, in Barker, *The Austin Papers*, III, pp. 135-136.

[11]Zavala to Austin, Sept. 17, 1835, in Zavala Papers, as quoted by Estep, *Lorenzo de Zavala*, p. 297.

the federal basis of the constitution of 1824, opposed that document's consecration of the religious and military *fueros* (special privileges), its religious intolerance, and its provisions of agreement with the Papacy. Zavala went on to predict that Santa Anna would only precipitate his own downfall if he committed the indiscretion of invading Texas. Zavala felt that Texas, with its rivers, forests, deserts, rifles, different language, and above all, its American perseverance, would combine to defeat the dictator.[12] In this analysis of the military situation Zavala was indeed flattering the relatively small group of English-speaking Texans as against the numerically superior Mexican army. Events, however, were to justify Zavala's respect for the Americans as fighters.

At the end of September 1835 Zavala was in San Felipe, working in collaboration with Stephen F. Austin and others in preparation for the forthcoming meeting for consultation. Before the consultation met, however, a skirmish at the town of Gonzales between the invading *santannistas* and the Texans on October 2, 1835 inaugurated the war that led to the independence of Texas.

Nathaniel W. Stephenson refers to the skirmish at Gonzales as "Lexington and Concord over again."[13] Simply stated, Colonel Domingo de Ugartechea, the *santannista comandante* of Texas, sent a corporal and four men to the Texan town of Gonzales to seize a six-pounder brass cannon that the town had had for four years as protection against the Indians. The *alcalde* (mayor) of Gonzales, Andrew Ponton, refused to turn over the weapon. Instead, he sent a letter of explanation to Colonel Ugartechea.

In reply to Ponton's letter, Colonel Ugartechea sent a force of *santannista* soldiers under Lieutenant Francisco Castañeda to take the cannon. Up and down the valleys of the Colorado and the Brazos went the appeal of Gonzales for aid. The Texan "minutemen" left their homesteads and hurried to Gonzales. On

---

[12]*Ibid.*
[13]*Texas and the Mexican War* (New Haven: Yale University Press, 1921), p. 61.

October 2, 1835 the two forces, consisting of a few hundred men, met. The *santannistas* were scattered, and a war had begun.

At this point a short recapitulation will bring the events into clearer focus. In brief, a number of Mexican states, including Yucatán, Zacatecas, and Coahuila y Texas, refused to abandon the Mexican federal constitution of 1824. They refused to accept Santa Anna's Plan of Cuernavaca, his overthrow of the federal republic and its constitution, and his assumption of dictatorial power under the frame of a new centralized government. Unfortunately for the *federalistas*, Santa Anna was able to deal with them separately, as they did not put up a united front. The Texans did, however, cling to the hope that they would receive aid from the other Mexican *federalistas* in support of the constitution of 1824 and against Santa Anna's innovations. To some extent they were successful.

Lorenzo de Zavala, former President of the General Constituent Congress of Mexico, former governor of the state of Mexico, former treasury minister, and former minister to France, joined the Texans. Zavala was to be the first vice president *ad interim* of the Republic of Texas. Colonel José Antonio Mexía (Mejía) fitted out an ill-fated expedition at New Orleans to lead against the *santannistas* in Tampico. Juan N. Seguín and Salvador Flores, Mexican-Texans from San Antonio de Béxar, led local Mexican-Texan troops against the *santannistas*. Also, Governor Agustín de Viesca of Coahuila y Texas, after his escape, joined the Texan *federalistas*.[14]

[14]Stephen F. Austin to Thomas F. McKinney, Dec. 16, 1835, in Barker, *The Austin Papers*, III, p. 285. This letter mentions Zavala, Mexía, and Viesca as being on the Texan side.

4
Federalism Destroyed

On October 3, 1835 the *santannista* congress in Mexico City gave the final stroke to the old federal system by making the states into mere departments in a centralized Mexico under the military dictatorship of General Antonio López de Santa Anna. In spite of Santa Anna's attempt to give the war in Texas the character of a national crusade against rebellious foreigners, the fact remains that it was Santa Anna who overthrew the Mexican federal constitution of 1824 and his troops who invaded Texas.

In his memoirs, *Mi Historia Militar y Política, 1810-1879; Memorias Ineditas,* Santa Anna conveniently ignores the fact that the Texans had been invited as colonists into the old Viceroyalty of New Spain by the Spanish government. Instead, the Texans are portrayed as ingrates and rebels against a benevolent Mexico that had granted them more privileges than they deserved. The Texans, according to Santa Anna, when not granted still greater privileges, thereupon rebelled.[1]

[1] Mexico City: Editoria Nacional, 1958; originally published by Genaro García and Carlos Pereyra in 1905, pp. 32-33.

It should be noted that in his memoirs Santa Anna twists the facts and fails to cite any specific privileges that he alleges the Texans were claiming. Furthermore, he erroneously refers to General Martín Perfecto de Cós as Commandant General of Texas, rather than Commandant General of the Eastern Interior States. Santa Anna also refers to the State of Texas rather than to the state of Coahuila y Texas. Significantly, the dictator does not call Texas a department of Mexico, as Mexico and her apologists were later wont to do.[2]

Interestingly, also, Justin Harvey Smith, in *The Annexation of Texas,* states that the flag that flew over the Alamo when Santa Anna attacked the Texans was the Mexican flag of the federal republic of 1824.[3]

Only when the usurper, Antonio López de Santa Anna, had destroyed even the remotest possibility that the Texans, in conjunction with other Mexican *federalistas,* could restore the old order, did the Texans opt for independence. Until the last, Stephen F. Austin and the Texans tried to cooperate with the remnants of the *federalista* party to support, and then to resurrect, the Mexican federal constitution of 1824. To accept the *santannista* decree of October 3, 1835, which converted the old states of the Mexican federal union into mere departments, meant the end of Texas.

José de Vasconcelos, a 20th-century Mexican historian, points out that the Texans did not initiate the war that led to their independence. Vasconcelos says:

> The Texans did not start it. When Santa Anna dissolved the legislature of Coahuila y Texas, the region remained, together with the rest of the country, without any other authority than the strong boot of the soldier.

Vasconcelos also labels Lorenzo de Zavala as the apparent inspirer of Texan independence and continues:

[2]*Ibid.*

[3]New York: Macmillan, 1941, corrected edition; originally published by Baker, 1911, p. 12. Hereafter cited as Smith, *The Annexation of Texas.*

The dispute over federalism gave the pretext; the hidden motives of Zavala were his personal hatred of Santa Anna and the interests he had acquired in Texas.

Finally, Vasconcelos thoroughly repudiates the idea that the Texan war for independence was perpetrated solely by the Texan settlers. He states:

> The presence of Zavala and of other Mexicans who, fugitives from the military régime, joined the North Americans in order to proclaim the independence of Texas, and to impose it . . .[4]

Vasconcelos also mentions the independent Republic of Yucatán, which existed for a few years in opposition to Santa Anna. Yucatán, incidentally, broke away from Mexico in 1841; rejoined Mexico in 1843; and revolted again and declared its neutrality between the United States and Mexico during the Mexican War. The state of Campeche likewise proclaimed itself neutral during the Mexican War. Ultimately, however, both states were reunited with Mexico.

It should now be obvious that, once the *federalista* party was defeated in the rest of Mexico, except for faraway Yucatán, Texas had but two options: (1) to submit to the dictator and be crushed or (2) to seek independence.

Before choosing independence, however, the Texans preferred to harbor as long as possible the illusion that the Mexican *federalistas* might gain control of the northern Mexican states and set up a northern confederacy. Under Stephen F. Austin's influence, the Texan consultation on November 7, 1835 adopted a declaration of causes for taking up arms against Santa Anna. In this declaration the Texans squarely put the blame on Santa Anna. The preamble and first article read:

DECLARATION OF THE PEOPLE OF TEXAS IN GENERAL CONVENTION ASSEMBLED.

[4]José de Vasconcelos, *Breve Historia de México, Edición Contemporanea, 1956* (Mexico City: Cia Editorial Continental, S.A., 1959, 4th ed.; 1st ed. in 1956), pp. 329-330.

Whereas, General Antonio Lopez de Santa Anna and other Military Chieftains have, by force of arms, overthrown the Federal Institutions of Mexico, and dissolved the Social Compact which existed between Texas and the other Members of the Mexican Confederacy—Now, the good People of Texas, availing themselves of their natural rights,

SOLEMNLY DECLARE

1st. That they have taken up arms in defence of their rights and Liberties, which were threatened by the encroachments of military despots, and in defence of the Republican Principles of the Federal Constitution of Mexico of eighteen hundred and twenty-four.[5]

The fifth article, perhaps, is even more significant:

5th. That they hold it to be their right, during the disorganization of the Federal System and the reign of despotism, to withdraw from the Union, to establish an independent Government, or to adopt such measures as they may deem best calculated to protect their rights and liberties; but that they will continue faithful to the Mexican Government so long as that nation is governed by the Constitution and Laws that were formed for the government of the Political Association.[6]

The advantage of the fifth article was that if the *federalistas* should win, Texas could remain a state of Mexico. On the other hand, in the event of a *santannista* victory, it would serve as a declaration of independence.

Regarding Texas' right to independence, Stephen F. Austin continued to take the position that the union with Mexico had

[5] From "Declaration of the People of Texas in General Convention Assembled," *Journals of the Consultation Held at San Felipe de Austin, Oct. 16, 1835* (Houston, 1838), pp. 21-22, as quoted in Ernest Wallace and David Martell Vigness (Eds.), *Documents of Texas History* (Austin: Steck, 1960; 1963 ed.), p. 91. Hereafter cited as Wallace and Vigness, *Documents of Texas History.*

[6] *Ibid.*

been dissolved by the overthrow of the federal constitution of 1824 without the consent of the people of Texas. The fact of independence was to be proven by the failure of Santa Anna's invasion and his signing of the Treaty of Velasco, recognizing the independence of Texas.

The good faith of the Texans and their loyalty to Mexico are easily demonstrated by the very consultation that issued the Texas declaration of causes for taking up arms against Santa Anna. On November 8, 1835 the consultation provided for the translation of its declaration into Spanish for distribution among their Mexican fellow citizens. The loyalty of the Texans to Mexico was further manifested when they organized their provisional government. Article X of the *Plan and Powers of the Provisional Government of Texas* states:

> Article X. Every officer and member of the Provisional Government, before entering upon the duties of his office, shall take and subscribe the following oath of office: "I, A.B., do solemnly swear (or affirm) that I will support the republican principles of the Constitution of Mexico of 1824 . . ."[7]

Also, it might be pointed out that, in organizing their government, the Texans called their chief executive "governor" instead of "president."[8] This was done because they still, at this late date, considered themselves as a part of the Mexican union, albeit the Mexico of the federal constitution of 1824.

On December 11, 1835 the Texans, under the command of General Edward Burleson, defeated the *santannista* invader, General Martín Perfecto de Cós, at San Antonio de Béxar. As part of his surrender agreement, General Cós was permitted to withdraw his army from Texas.

Three of the articles in the capitulation that the Texans

[7] From *Ordinances and Decrees of the Consultation, Provisional Government of Texas and the Convention, Which Assembled at Washington March 1, 1836* (Houston, 1838), pp. 4-13, as quoted in Wallace and Vigness (Eds.), *Documents of Texas History*, p. 93.

[8] *Ibid.*, p. 92.

compelled General Cós to sign are important enough to be reproduced. They are the first, third, and fourteenth:[9]

> 1st. That General Cos and his officers retire with their arms and private property *into the interior of the Republic,* under parole of honor that they will not in any way oppose the establishment of the Federal [Mexican] Constitution of 1824.
>
> 3d. That the General take the *convicts* lately brought in by Colonel Ugartechea *beyond the Rio Grande.*
>
> 14th. General Burleson will furnish General Cos with such provisions as can be obtained necessary for his troops *to the Rio Grande,* at the ordinary price of the country.

By the first article in the capitulation the Texans once more showed their loyalty to the Mexican federal constitution of 1824. In the third and fourteenth articles it can be seen that the Texans had revolted with a view to making the Rio Grande their southwestern boundary, and not the Nueces, a point that will be pursued in more depth in Chapter 6.

At any rate, with the departure of the defeated General Cós below the Rio Grande, Texas had won its right to existence on the battlefield.

Santa Anna, however, was determined to add Texas to his dictatorship. The usurper reacted to the defeat of General Cós with a decree that all foreigners who might be caught under arms on Mexican soil should be treated as pirates and shot. The effect of Santa Anna's decree was to confirm the conviction of the Texans that they were engaged in a war to save themselves from a military despotism. It also served to strengthen the determination of many Americans to come to the assistance of the beleagured Texans.

When, in conjunction with the new decree, Santa Anna lined up nearly 400 prisoners of war at Goliad on March 27, 1836 and had them shot in cold blood, even the dullest Texans were forced to realize that it was independence or death. This point was not

[9]United States Congress, *Appendix To The Congressional Globe,* 30th Congress, 1st session, June 5, 1848, p. 660.

lost on the Mexican General Vicente Filisola, who criticized Santa Anna's conduct of the Texas Campaign:

A worse evil resulted from this inconsiderate and inhumane conduct [of Santa Anna], and from the butcheries of San Patricio, el Refugio, Goliad, and Guadalupe Victoria, which is, that all the [Texan] colonists, good and evil, were made to understand that their cause had no other remedy than to win, die, or abandon the country forever; whereas with a more humane and considerate power, without spilling so much blood, the end of the war would have been without doubt happy; Texas would not have been demoralized, and any motive for imputations of barbarity against the [Mexican] nation would have been avoided.[10]

By now it was equally obvious that the possibility of assistance from the Mexican *federalistas* in defense of the Mexican federal constitution of 1824 was an illusion. Santa Anna had triumphed everywhere except in Texas and far-away Yucatán. Santa Anna, by the Plan of Cuernavaca and the overthrow of the Mexican federal constitution of 1824, had destroyed the old Mexican union. By resorting to the sword, he had severed any remaining link between his régime and the Texans.

---

[10]Vicente Filisola, *Memorias para la historia de la Guerra de Tejas* (Mexico City: Imprenta de Ignacio Cumplido, 1849), p. 128. Hereafter cited as Filisola, *Memorias de la Guerra de Tejas*.

5

Texan Independence

On March 6, 1836 General Antonio López de Santa Anna, President of Mexico and self-styled Napoleon of the West, won a Pyrrhic victory at the Alamo. With 3000 men under his command, Santa Anna had finally defeated and butchered 187 Texans. Four days earlier, on March 2, unknown to both the *santannistas* and the defenders of the Alamo, Texas had declared its independence from Mexico.

With the official declaration of independence, the anti-Santa Anna Mexicans were forced to choose between Texas and Mexico. The most prominent Mexican *federalista* who chose to stay with Texas was Lorenzo de Zavala. On the other hand, the most prominent Mexican *federalista* to desert the Texan cause was former Vice President Valentín Gómez Farías.

On March 17 David G. Burnet was elected *ad interim* President of Texas and Lorenzo de Zavala *ad interim* Vice President. The election of Zavala to the vice presidency of Texas symbolized the unity of the Texan people, both American and Mexican, against the Santa Anna dictatorship.

On April 21, 1836 the Texan army, under the command of General Sam Houston, defeated General Santa Anna at the battle of San Jacinto. Santa Anna, furthermore, was captured by the victorious Texans.

On May 14, 1836 by the Treaty of Velasco Mexico recognized the independence of Texas. Herein lies the key to subsequent disputes. Mexican historians and those who take the Mexican side argue that Santa Anna, now a prisoner of war, could not speak for Mexico. The fact is, however, that General Antonio López de Santa Anna was still the President of Mexico. Ironically, this very fact facilitated his discovery by the Texans as a prisoner in their hands. When a disguised Santa Anna was led into the Texan camp, the *santannista* soldiers who were now prisoners of war saw through the disguise and shouted: *"El presidente!"* Moreover, however repugnantly the Texans may have viewed Santa Anna's assumption of power, he was *de facto* if not *de jure* not only president, but the unquestioned dictator. The Texans, by striking out for independence instead of continuing to champion the Mexican federal constitution of 1824, were recognizing the fact of that document's demise and the assumption of power by Santa Anna. The dictator needed no congressional approval of his actions. Until he was removed from office, which did not take place until almost a year *after* news of his defeat and *after* the Treaty of Velasco had reached Mexico City, Santa Anna, and he alone, spoke for Mexico.

Santa Anna's power, even while a prisoner of war, was undisputed. This is proven by the fact that his orders to General Vicente Filisola were obeyed. With the defeat of the *santannista* troops under the direct command of Santa Anna, the task of subjugating Texas fell to General Filisola, who commanded a second *santannista* army in Texas. Starting on April 27, 1836, General Filisola began receiving orders from the prisoner-dictator, Santa Anna. General Filisola was first ordered to retire from Texas and later to exchange prisoners with the Texans, in accordance with the provisions of the Treaty of Velasco.

The Treaty of Velasco, as already stated, was signed on May 14, 1836. The key signatories were the two presidents, General Antonio López de Santa Anna of Mexico and David G. Burnet of Texas. In addition to recognizing the independence of Texas, the Treaty of Velasco accepted the Rio Grande as the Mexican-Texan boundary.[1]

As General Vicente Filisola was in command of a second *santannista* army in Texas, it was deemed desirable to have him sign the Treaty of Velasco. This was accomplished by sending Colonel Benjamin F. Smith and Captain Henry Teal to General Filisola in order to obtain his signature. On May 26, 1836 General Filisola and two of his subordinates, General Eugenio Tolsa and Colonel Agustín Amat, signed the Treaty of Velasco.[2] Making General Filisola a signatory to the Treaty of Velasco was also desirable because his name appeared in the treaty itself. Article 8 of the public agreement states:

> Article 8. By express, to be immediately despatched, this agreement shall be sent to General Filisola, and to General T. J. Rusk, commander of the Texan army, in order that they may be apprized of its stipulations; and, to this end, they will exchange engagements to comply with the same.[3]

General Filisola, incidentally, was not a prisoner of war.

Once Filisola had recrossed the Rio Grande and retired from Texas in accordance with the provisions of the Treaty of Velasco, he faced an irate government in Mexico City. The various Mexican generals who had in any way participated in, or been responsible for, the ill-fated invasion of Texas, tried to blame each other for the disastrous results.

General José Urrea, in particular, charged that General Filisola had accorded the Texans the recognition of a government.[4] In defense of his actions, General Filisola stated:

[1]Chapter 6, immediately following, will discuss the boundary.

[2]Filisola, *Memorias de la Guerra de Tejas*, p. 306; Vicente Filisola, *Evacuation of Texas* (Waco, Texas: Texian Press, 1965: Translation of the Representation Addressed to the Supreme Government by General Vicente Filisola in defense of his honor, August 19, 1836 (translated by George Louis Hammeken in 1837, edited by James M. Day in 1965), p. 58. Hereafter cited as Filisola, *Evacuation of Texas*.

[3]Wallace and Vigness (Eds.), *Documents of Texas History*, p. 117.

[4]Filisola, *Evacuation of Texas*, p. 6.

. . . only in a war where no quarter was to be given, by an especial and positive order from the government, could I be prohibited the exchange of prisoners. And to what else did I compromise myself in recognizing that treaty [of Velasco] than to retreat and exchange prisoners?[5]

Whatever General Filisola might have wished to imply by this comment, the fact remains that he was a signatory to the Treaty of Velasco. Furthermore, far from trying to hide this fact, in his memoirs on the Texas Campaign he himself lists his own name along with those of Eugenio Tolsa, Agustín Amat, Henry Teal, and Benjamin F. Smith as having signed the Treaty of Velasco at the stream of Mugerero on May 26, 1836.[6]

Filisola also admitted that Mexico had lost Texas irrevocably:

. . . Mexico had lost it [Texas] forever, due to the anxiety and indiscretion of the general-in-chief [Santa Anna], who wasn't content with only punishment . . . but who wanted to exterminate them [the Texans] forever.[7]

Regarding any charge that General Filisola had acted incorrectly in signing the Treaty of Velasco or in attempting to exchange prisoners of war, he is completely vindicated by the facts. In the first place, he was obeying his superior, President Antonio López de Santa Anna. Second, he had received a communication from General José María Tornel y Mendivil, then Minister of War in Mexico City, which granted him discretionary powers and specifically urged him to exchange prisoners of war. The communication from Tornel read in part:

The fate of all the prisoners is very interesting to the nation, and it is recommended to your Excellency to endeavor to alleviate it, *giving authority from this moment to propose exchanges, and to preserve for this purpose, and because humanity exacts it, the life of the*

[5]*Ibid.*, p. 14.
[6]Filisola, *Memorias de la Guerra de Tejas*, p. 306; Filisola, *Evacuation of Texas*, p. 58.
[7]Filisola, *Memorias de la Guerra de Tejas*, p. 132.

prisoners made, and that may be made from the enemy. Your Excellency knows the circumstances which may result from an imprudence committed in this affair; but the government fears nothing as regards this, because it knows how great is the skill and zeal of your Excellency, for the best service of the country.[8]

It might also be pointed out that General Filisola was completely exonerated at his court-martial.[9]

The Treaty of Velasco, by which Mexico recognized the independence of Texas, provides a key to understanding the truth about the subsequent war between Mexico and the United States. It is therefore necessary that its validity be accepted.

The Mexican school of historians who reject the validity of the treaty on the ground that Santa Anna was a prisoner of war at the time and hence, in their opinion, incapable of speaking for Mexico, are apparently or conveniently unaware of the Spanish precedent of dealing with prisoners of war. In 1525, King François I of France was defeated and captured at the battle of Pavia by King Carlos I of Spain, Charles V of the Holy Roman Empire. To obtain his freedom, the French king signed the Treaty of Madrid (1526), in which he renounced territorial claims in Italy, Flanders, Artois, and Burgundy. The Treaty of Madrid (1526) was subsequently reaffirmed by the Treaty of Cambria (1529).

Furthermore, as already stated, Santa Anna was no mere constitutional president who needed congressional confirmation of his actions. Bluntly speaking, he was Mexico incarnate. Santa Anna's power over Mexico is demonstrated by the fact that he was not deposed after his defeat at the battle of San Jacinto or after signing the Treaty of Velasco. Santa Anna remained *el presidente,* while his puppet, José Justo Corro, was merely the *presidente interino* (president *ad interim*) in the absence of the dictator.

[8]General José María Tornel y Mendivil to General Vicente Filisola, May 15, 1836, in Filisola, *Evacuation of Texas*, p. 55.

[9]Thomas W. Streeter, *Bibliography of Texas, 1795-1845*, Part II (of a three-part series), *Mexican Imprints Relating to Texas, 1803-1845* (Cambridge: Harvard University Press, 1956), pp. 144-145.

During Santa Anna's absence, and in view of the weakness of Justo Corro, the dominant member of the *santannista* government was General José María Tornel y Mendívil, the war minister. Both Justo Corro and Tornel remained steadfast *santannistas*. Both were considered by congressional leaders to be more concerned for their master's freedom and good name than with the loss of Texas itself.[10]

When Santa Anna's defeat was made known to the public, Justo Corro, in an executive decree, pleaded for unity and a cessation of domestic strife. An anonymous pamphlet, *Proceso del general Santa Anna,* which appeared shortly after the battle of San Jacinto, blamed Santa Anna for the loss of Texas and lamented that Mexico was governed by Santa Anna's puppet congress. The pamphlet even described the deputies and senators as "reptiles" who had dragged themselves "at the feet of the tyrant."[11]

When General Tornel announced to the Mexican congress the news of Santa Anna's good fortune in obtaining his release from the generous Texans, the congress preferred to remain silent. Santa Anna's release and imminent return to Mexico nevertheless necessitated some clarification of his status on the part of the government. The executive department, headed by José Justo Corro and General José María Tornel y Mendívil, maintained that Santa Anna was indeed the president.[12] A number of congressmen, however, perhaps emboldened by the election in January 1837 of General Anastasio Bustamante to the presidency and his pending inauguration on April 19, were now willing to question whether Santa Anna was still president.

In February 1837, a committee of the Mexican congress took upon itself the task of determining Santa Anna's status. In view of the election of a new president the previous month for the term beginning April 19, 1837, the action of the congressmen against the lame-duck president can be understood only as a fear

[10]Manuel Urbina Jr., "The Impact of the Texas Revolution on the Government and Politics of Mexico, 1836-1838," M.A. Thesis, University of Texas, 1967, p. 23; hereafter cited as Urbina, "Impact of Texas on Mexico."

[11]*Proceso del general Santa Anna* (Mexico City: Impreso por Francisco Torres, 1836), p.2, as quoted in Urbina, "Impact of Texas on Mexico," p. 27.

[12]*El Cosmopolita* (Mexico City), Feb. 15, 1837, p. 4.

of Santa Anna. Apparently many of his erstwhile supporters had taken advantage of the master's absence and now feared the effects of his return to power, even briefly. Possibly they feared that, once reinstated in power, Santa Anna would set aside the recent election of a successor and invalidate whatever advantages they hoped to obtain from the new president-elect.

Congressman Pedro Ahumada, for one, was displeased by the kangaroo justice by which many congressmen were planning to strip Santa Anna of the presidency. Ahumada stated:

> If General Santa Anna still is president, or at least still enjoys the prerogatives of this magistracy, why aren't legal means used to judge him? Make the accusation, form the corresponding summary, have congress convene itself as a grand jury and make the corresponding declaration, and then it will have an appearance of legality. But to deprive a man of his rights, of his employment and insignia of office without hearing him, and for the Congress which absolutely is not able nor ought to do it? This appears to me to be illegal, imprudent, unjust; for these reasons I have voted against the judgment, as much in general as in this particular case . . .[13]

The editor of *El Cosmopolita* also supported Santa Anna's legal rights, while stressing his own anti*santannista* position.[14]

In spite of Congressman Pedro Ahumada's logic and of the legalities involved, the anti*santannista* faction was to score a victory. Led by Congressman Carlos María Bustamante, the opponents of Santa Anna voted on February 22, 1837 to strip him retroactively of the presidency as of December 30, 1836. The vote was 40 to 23.

Congressman Bustamante's resolution officially stated:

> It is declared that General D. Antonio López de Santa Anna ceased to be president upon the publication of the new constitutional laws.[15]

[13]*Ibid.*, Feb. 22, 1837, p. 5.
[14]*Ibid.*, Feb. 8, 1837, p. 4.
[15]*Ibid.*, Feb. 22, 1837, p. 6.

Ironically, when Santa Anna on October 3, 1835 overthrew the Constitution of 1824, his puppet congress drew up a new set of constitutional laws. These laws were published on December 30, 1836. As Santa Anna was not present in Mexico City at that time, he was unable to swear allegiance to the new decrees. It was on these superficial grounds that he was officially deposed.

It should be emphasized at this point that Santa Anna, as president of Mexico, signed the Treaty of Velasco on May 14, 1836. He was not deposed until February 22, 1837 by an ex-post-facto resolution that retroactively deprived him of the presidency as of December 30, 1836.

Added to the above, we have the discretionary authorization of War Minister Tornel to General Vicente Filisola, and Filisola's signing of the treaty of Velasco. It should further be emphasized that General Filisola, who was not a prisoner of war and who also signed the Treaty of Velasco, was exonerated at his court-martial. The worst indictment hurled against Filisola, as already stated, was General José Urrea's charge that Filisola had accorded the Texans recognition as a government.

Finally, from October 3, 1835, when Santa Anna overthrew the federal constitution of 1824, until December 30, 1836, when the new constitution was promulgated, there was no constitution in effect in Mexico. As already quoted, in the words of the contempory Mexican historian, José de Vasconcelos, Mexico was "without any other authority than the strong boot of the soldier." That soldier was General Antonio López de Santa Anna, and his signature on the Treaty of Velasco was the signature of Mexico.

The fact that the Mexican authorities who subsequently replaced Santa Anna refused to accept the Treaty of Velasco does not in any way detract from its validity.

The Mexicans and the pro-Mexican historians who reject the Treaty of Velasco have no qualms about accepting the Treaty of Córdoba (1821) as a bona fide recognition of Mexican independence by Spain. It will be remembered, however, that the Treaty of Córdoba was negotiated by the Spanish Captain General, Juan O'Donojú, and the Mexican rebel, Agustín de

Iturbide. This so-called treaty was promptly rejected by King Fernando VII of Spain, and the disgraced O'Donojú, who had so flagrantly exceeded his authority, dared not return to Spain. O'Donojú subsequently died in Mexico with the rebels.

It was only on December 28, 1836, by the Treaty of Madrid, that Spain deigned to recognize the Mexican rebels who controlled a part of the old Viceroyalty of New Spain. By December 28, 1836, of course, Texas was no longer associated with Mexico. The best that the Mexican school of historians can logically claim is that, until December 28, 1836, neither Mexico nor Texas was a legitimate state. By the reasoning applied by the Mexican school to the Treaty of Velasco, both Mexico and Texas were, at the time of that treaty, rebellious sections of the Viceroyalty of New Spain. To follow such a line of thought, however, would be to say that Mexico never held any sovereignty over Texas. Even while Texas and Mexico were associated from 1821 to 1836, they were merely associates in rebellion against Spain. The Mexicans cannot have their tequila and drink it at the same time!

The Mexicans, in trying to date their own independence from the so-called Treaty of Córdoba, can claim that they had obtained international recognition from foreign powers, such as the United States, Great Britain, and France. Coincidentally, the Republic of Texas soon obtained international recognition from these same foreign powers. The Mexicans might also claim that they held *de facto* control of their section of the Viceroyalty of New Spain and by the law of *uti possidetis* did indeed exercise sovereignty. This claim would be questionable at best, in view of the frequent internal wars and revolutions and the breakaway of various territories, unless the Mexicans were referring only to the central valley around the capital. In relying on the law of *uti possidetis*, however, the Mexicans would be admitting the legitimacy of the Republic of Texas, as that republic did indeed control the territory north of the Rio Grande.

In summation, this chapter has shown that the independence of Texas was an established deed, as attested by the inability of the arms of Mexico to conquer her. The Treaty of

Velasco, which recognized this independence, has been shown to be legitimate and bona fide. General Vicente Filisola, a signatory of the Treaty of Velasco, further recognized this independence when he admitted that Texas was lost forever.

In the last analysis it should be pointed out that all treaties are signed under duress on the part of the defeated. In this respect, Santa Anna was no different from any other defeated chieftain.

6
The Texas Boundary

As was pointed out in Chapter 5, Texas established her *de facto* independence on the battlefield of San Jacinto on April 21, 1836. This independence was then recognized by General Antonio López de Santa Anna, the president of Mexico, by the Treaty of Velasco on May 14, 1836. Also, General Vicente Filisola, who succeeded Santa Anna as general-in-chief of the Mexican forces in the Texas theater, signed the Treaty of Velasco on May 26, 1836 and retired beyond the Rio Grande.

Unfortunately, Santa Anna's successors in Mexico City preferred to deprecate the Treaty of Velasco and deny its validity. At the time they were denying the independence of Texas, however, the Mexican leaders were nevertheless maintaining that the true Mexican-Texas boundary was the Nueces rather than the Rio Grande. It will be left to the Mexicans to explain how a non-existent republic could still have a boundary.

Shortly after the signing of the Treaty of Velasco the Mexican authorities placed General José Urrea in command of the army to conquer Texas. When General Urrea failed, the command went to General Juan V. Amador. After General Amador's failure, General Nicolás Bravo was named general-in-chief. When General Bravo failed to conquer Texas, the war minister, General José María Tornel y Mendívil, gave General

Vicente Filisola a second chance to conquer that tough little republic. On May 15, 1837, General Filisola was appointed by War Minister Tornel as general-in-chief of the Mexican army in the North, with instructions to conquer Texas.

General Filisola, it will be recalled, had at the request of President Santa Anna signed the Treaty of Velasco and withdrawn his troops across the Rio Grande. For this General Filisola had been relieved of his command as general-in-chief of the Mexican forces in Texas, court-martialed, and forced to defend his actions, which he successfully did. Now, exonerated and rehabilitated, General Vicente Filisola was ordered to conquer Texas. Like the earlier Mexican attempts to conquer the republic, the Filisola campaign of 1837 ended in failure.

The failure of the Filisola campaign in 1837, furthermore, marked the last time the Mexicans seriously attempted to conquer Texas until the inception of the Mexican War with the United States, nine years later. In the interim there were periodic threats by Mexican generals, usually the incumbent president of Mexico or an aspirant for the presidency, to conquer Texas all the way to the Sabine River, the boundary between the United States and Texas.

One of the earliest such threats was made by General Anastasio Bustamante, President of Mexico, on September 28, 1837.[1] One of the last of these threats was that of General Mariano Paredes y Arrillaga on December 14, 1845, when he announced his rebellion against President José Joaquín de Herrera in his Plan de San Luis Potosí.[2]

Border warfare would result from these Mexican threats, as well as the temporary Mexican capture of San Antonio on two separate occasions in 1842 by General Adrian Woll. The Mexican incursions, however, proved as ineffective as the subsequent retaliatory incursions by the Texans on the southwestern side of the Rio Grande. Neither Mexico nor Texas was able to maintain itself on the enemy's side of the Rio Grande.

Mexico's assertion that the Texan boundary was the Nueces,

[1]*Telegraph and Texas Register* (Houston), Mar. 17, 1838.

[2]Frank D. Robertson, "The Military and Political Career of Mariano Paredes y Arrillaga, 1797-1849," Ph.D. dissertation, University of Texas, 1955, p. 193.

rather than the Rio Grande, had its inception in the Mexican federal constitution of 1824. Under that document the Nueces, rather than the Rio Grande, did indeed serve as the boundary between the states of Coahuila y Texas on the one side and Tamaulipas on the other. As was pointed out in Chapter 4, however, the dictator, General Antonio López de Santa Anna, nullified the federal constitution of 1824. That document thus ceased to have the force of law as far as the Mexican government was concerned, and Texas might be regarded as having reverted to its pre-1824 status as a separate entity, with its ancient boundaries. This meant that the union between Coahuila and Texas, which had never existed under Spain or Iturbide, was severed. It also meant that the southwestern boundary of Texas once again extended across the Nueces, as it had under both Spain and Iturbide's Mexican Empire.

According to *The Congressional Globe*, the southwestern boundary of the old Spanish province of Texas had been the Rio Grande. Most cartographers agree, however, that the boundary between the Spanish provinces of Texas and Nuevo Santander was neither the Nueces nor the Rio Grande, but rather a line in between.[3] The province of Nuevo Santander, incidentally, no longer existed; most of its territory had been supplanted by Santa Anna's new "department" of Tamaulipas.

Furthermore, much of the territory of the Republic of Texas that Mexico claimed lay between the Rio Grande and the Pecos River, not the Nueces. This section had belonged to the former Spanish province of Coahuila and more recently to the state of Coahuila y Texas. Concerning this territory, the Republic of Texas had an additional claim, as it could legitimately be viewed as the successor to the combined state of Coahuila y Texas.

Following this particular line of reasoning, it will be remembered that, as pointed out in Chapter 3, Governor Agustín de Viesca, the last governor of Coahuila y Texas, had resisted the

---

[3]United States Congress, *Appendix To The Congressional Globe*, 29th Congress, 1st session, June 29, 1846, p. 803; William R. Shepherd, *Historical Atlas* (New York: Barnes & Noble, 1964, 9th ed.; originally published in 1956), pp. 198-199; R. F. Treharne & Harold Fullard, Ed., *Muir's Historical Atlas, Ancient and Classical.* (London: George Philip, 1971, reprint of 6th ed., originally published in 1938), p. 70.

attempt of Santa Anna and his cohort, General Martín Perfecto de Cós, to destroy his state. The state legislature, in addition, had authorized Governor Viesca to move the seat of government at his discretion in order prevent it from falling into the hands of the *santannistas*. Governor Viesca had been captured, but after his escape had joined the Texans.

The Republic of Texas, then, might alternatively be seen as the rump of the old state of Coahuila y Texas and thus entitled to all the territory of that former entity on both sides of the Rio Grande!

The Texans, however, were apparently satisfied with the natural boundary of the Rio Grande. As pointed out in Chapter 4, when the Texans revolted they did so with a view to the Rio Grande as their southwestern boundary. This was demonstrated by the capitulation agreement they forced General Cós to sign, whereby he retreated across the Rio Grande.

Furthermore, in the Treaty of Velasco, whereby Mexico recognized the independence of the Republic of Texas, the Rio Grande was indicated as the Mexican-Texas boundary on two separate occasions: 1. Article 3 of the public agreement: "The Mexican troops will evacuate the territory of Texas, passing to the other side of the Rio Grande del Norte,"[4] and 2. Article 4 of the secret agreement: "A treaty of commerce, amity, and limits, will be established between Mexico and Texas, the territory of the latter not to extend beyond the Rio Bravo [Rio Grande] del Norte."[5]

In spite of Mexican claims that Texas did not extend beyond the Nueces, the contrary is easily shown. Texan settlements, the most notable of which was Corpus Christi, were located beyond the Nueces. Most of the territory between the Nueces and the Rio Grande, however, was uninhabited. This was the area called *El Desierto Muerto* by both the Spaniards and the Mexicans, which translates into The Dead Desert. More poetically, it is rendered The Desert of Death. The Texans called the region Wild Horse Desert.

[4]*Ibid.*, 30th Congress, 1st session, Jan. 12, 1848, p. 95; Wallace and Vigness, *Documents of Texas History*, p. 117.

[5]Wallace and Vigness, *Documents of Texas History,* p. 117.

This region was intentionally left deserted by the Texans as a part of their military strategy. On August 8, 1836 David G. Burnet, the President *ad interim* of Texas, inaugurated the Texan policy that a wasteland should separate the population of Texas from the Mexicans beyond the Rio Grande.[6] On that date President Burnet authorized R. R. Royall to raise a company of "Independent Rangers" to gather in the large herds of cattle and horses between the Nueces and the Rio Grande that "have no ostensible owner and many of which are supposed to belong to Mexican citizens resident beyond the Rio Grande."[7]

The purpose of President Burnet's order was that, if and when war with Mexico should be renewed, it would be difficult for the Mexican army to cross an empty wasteland from which the cattle and horses had been driven off.[8] Also, the supply of cattle and horses for the Texan army would be increased. Should the Mexicans succeed in marching an army across The Desert of Death without finding supplies en route, the soldiers would probably not be fit for immediate duty because of fatigue from having transported quantities of provisions so far across a hot wasteland.

Joseph Milton Nance, referring to the country around the Nueces in *After San Jacinto: The Texas-Mexican Frontier, 1836-1841*, states: "The only civilized settlements were at [San Antonio de] Béxar, Goliad, and Refugio, all well east of the Nueces . . ."[9] The area between the Nueces and the settlements along the banks of the Rio Grande was the abode of "herds of wild horses and cattle and almost every conceivable species of native animal, and was infested by thieves, robbers, and murderers."[10] It was this area that Texan President David G. Burnet wished to clear of its wild livestock.

[6]David G. Burnet to R. R. Royall, Aug. 8, 1836, in Texas, *Executive Department Journals, March 1836-September 1836*, pp. 139-140; same to same, in William C. Binkley (Ed.), *Official Correspondence of the Texas Revolution, 1835-1836* (New York: Vanderbilt University, 1936), II, pp. 912-913. Hereafter cited as Binkley, *Official Correspondence*.

[7]*Ibid.*

[8]*Ibid.*

[9]Joseph Milton Nance, *After San Jacinto: The Texas-Mexican Frontier, 1836-1841* (Austin: Univ. of Texas Press, 1963), p. 4. Hereafter cited as Nance, *After San Jacinto*.

[10]*Ibid.*, p. 5.

Texan cowboys, actually lawless frontiersmen, raided the area west of the Nueces and drove out the cattle from those Mexican ranches that existed in that area.[11] Furthermore, these daring Texan cowboys often expanded their activities and extended their raids as far from the Nueces River as the towns of Laredo, Guerrero, and Matamoros, the latter two beyond the border on the Mexican side of the Rio Grande. The Texan cowboys were not particular in distinguishing between wild cattle and horses and those owned by Mexicans. They justified their actions under the "law of retaliation" for property that the Mexican army, in its retreat from Texas, had confiscated without compensation.

Nance conveniently lists the more famous cowboys who in effect dominated the region between the Nueces and the Rio Grande. They were, in the order Nance lists them: Captains A. T. Miles, J. C. Neill, ——— Merrell, William Wells, John T. Price, Jack (V.R.) Palmer, ——— Hull, W. J. Cairns (Scotch), John H. Yerby, James P. Ownsby, Jacob ("Jake") Hendricks (Pennsylvania Dutch), Ewen Cameron (Scotch), Samuel W. Jordan, and such lesser persons as "Tonkaway" Jones, Richard Roman, Joseph Dolan from Nacogdoches, Captain Thomas Hagler of Houston, Pierre (Peter) Rouche (Frenchman), Thomas Lyons (Irish), John Smith (Tennessean), James Taylor, Josiah Creed, John Hefferson (Irish), Mabry Gray, and "Big" (J? B?) Brown (from Missouri). Nance also mentions "and others numbering not less than three or four hundred."[12]

It should not be assumed that all these cowboys were murderers or that they stole from fellow Texans. Nance singles out only two such: "The parties led by Brown and Gray were regarded as murderers and cutthroats, and other parties had very little to do with them because of their atrocities."[13] Many of these cowboys, incidentally, are listed in the Mirabeau Buonaparte Lamar Papers, VI. Nance's list has been used merely for convenience.

[11]Thomas Jefferson Rusk to Alexander Somervell, June 22, 1836, in Binkley, *Official Correspondence*, II, pp. 810-811.

[12]Nance, *After San Jacinto*, p. 65.

[13]*Ibid.*

It will be noticed that none of the above names are of Spanish or Mexican origin; the point is that Texans, and not Mexicans, were in effective control of the northeastern bank of the Rio Grande. It is necessary to make this point as the Mexicans, and even some Americans such as Abraham Lincoln, were to raise the question of where the actual boundary between Mexico and Texas existed.

Far from controlling any territory northeast of the Rio Grande, the Mexican government was not even in control on its own side of that international border for periods of time. One such period was during the Federalist Wars (1838-1840), when *federalistas* battled *centralistas,* and the anti-government *federalistas* held large areas of northern Mexico. Another was following the defeat of the *federalistas* in 1840, when the *federalista* leaders Antonio Canales and Jesús Cárdenas set up the Republic of the Rio Grande.[14]

In view of the breakaway of the Central American region, including Guatemala and adjacent areas, after the collapse of the Iturbide régime, the independence of Texas, the off-again-on-again independence of Yucatán, the establishment of the Republic of the Rio Grande, and the quasi-independence of California,[15] one can indeed appreciate DeVoto's comment that " . . . it is a fundamental mistake to think of Mexico, in this period, or for many years before, as a republic or even a government. It must be understood as a late stage in the breakdown of the Spanish Empire."[16]

The fact is that Mexico, which had once been the center of a vast empire—the Viceroyalty of New Spain—stretching from the Philippines to Cuba, had degenerated into little more than a city-state in the valley of Anahuac. The authority of the generals who ruled Mexico City was lessened in direct proportion to the distance from the capital.

As this chapter marks the end of the transition of Texas from a province in the Viceroyalty of New Spain to an independent

[14]For more information on the Republic of the Rio Grande, see David Martell Vigness, "The Republic of the Rio Grande: An Example of Separatism in Northern Mexico." Ph.D. dissertation University of Texas, 1951.

[15]California will be dealt with in subsequent chapters.

[16]Bernard Devoto, *The Year of Decision: 1846* (Boston: Little, Brown, 1943), p. 13.

republic, with a definite frontier along the Rio Grande, a brief summary to this point is in order.

The first six chapters have illustrated a number of points concerning Texas. First, the Austin land grant, which brought the Texan-American settlers, antedated the creation of Mexico. It was granted by the Spanish *comandante general,* General Joaquín de Arredondo. Second, a number of the provinces of the Viceroyalty of New Spain, including Texas, formed a federal union and established a federal constitution in 1824. Third, this federal government was overthrown by a military dictator, General Antonio López de Santa Anna. Fourth, the overthrow of the Mexican federal constitution of 1824 and the reduction of the states comprising this federal union into departments was resisted by many Mexicans. Fifth, the Texans suffered repeatedly at the hands of the Mexicans. Sixth, the Texans were loyal Mexicans who supported the Mexican federal constitution of 1824. They resisted, however, the military despotism of a centralized state in which Santa Anna attempted to turn Texas into a mere department of Mexico. Seventh, Texas never was in fact a department of Mexico. Eighth, Santa Anna, by overthrowing the Mexican federal union, forced the Texans to choose between independence and submission to his despotism. Ninth, the Texan war for independence was supported by both English-speaking and Spanish-speaking Texans. It was not part of some plot by the English-speaking Texans to break away from Mexico, but evolved out of a civil war in defense of the Mexican federal constitution of 1824. Tenth, the Texans met Santa Anna's appeal to the sword, defeated him, and established an independent Republic of Texas. Eleventh, Mexico recognized the independence of Texas and the boundary of the Rio Grande in the Treaty of Velasco. Twelfth, the Treaty of Velasco was a legitimate and bona fide treaty. Thirteenth, the Rio Grande formed the historic Mexican-Texan boundary by reason of geography, law, and *de facto* control.

Once the independence of the Republic of Texas is thus viewed, it is obvious that Texas had the sovereign right to join the federal union of the United States, provided only that the United States was willing.

Texas around the time of the Mexican-American War

Money issued by the independent Republic of Texas during its period of independence.

General Parades and Cabinet receiving the news of the Brilliant Battles
of Palo Alto and Resaca de la Palma, from a Mexican Soldier.

New York Herald cartoonist pictures reaction of the Mexican government on learning of American victories (June 14, 1846 edition).

SCENE AT THE BATTLE OF THE RESACA DE LA PALMA

Just Before the Capture of General La Vera.

Newspaper illustrator depicts his version of the American victory in the Battle of the Resaca de la Palma.

NEW YORK, SUNDAY MORNING, APRIL 11, 1847.

APPEARANCE AT VERA CRUZ ON THE 29th OF MARCH, 1847,

When the American Flag was Hoisted over that City and over the Castle of San Juan de Ulua.

THE SALUTE FROM THE CASTLE AND AMERICAN FLEET.

New York Herald illustration of the American fleet at the captured Mexican City of Vera Cruz published by the newspaper April 11, 1847.

NEW YORK, FRIDAY MORNING, MAY 28, 1847.

THE MAIN PLAZA IN THE CITY OF MEXICO.

VIEW OF THE HALLS OF THE MONTEZUMAS.

A newspaper illustration of the Main Plaza of Mexico City, home of the defeated enemy.

PART II
Mexico and the United States

7
MEXICAN WAR THREATS

Starting with threats against the territorial integrity of the Republic of Texas, from the very birth of that republic the Mexican government increasingly threatened war against the United States as the possibility of American annexation of Texas gained momentum. On August 23, 1843 José María de Bocanegra, the Mexican Minister of Foreign Relations, wrote to the American Minister to Mexico, Waddy Thompson, on the subject of the possible union of Texas with the United States. Foreign Minister Bocanegra warned that the Mexican government would consider the incorporation of Texas into the territory of the United States as an American declaration of war against the Mexican republic. Bocanegra informed Thompson specifically that the Mexican president had ordered him to say

That the [Government] of Mexico considered as a declaration of war against the Mexican Republic the existence of that accord of the incorporation of Texas into the territory of the United States. The certainty of the fact [of annexation] would suffice that instantly war would be proclaimed [by Mexico against the United States], leaving to the civilized world the decision as to the justice of the Mexican people, in a struggle in which they [the Mexicans] were found so far from provoking.[1]

What bothered the Mexicans was that many Texans favored annexation to the United States. As early as November 1836 Texas had in fact voted in favor of joining the American Union. The Texan Secretary of State, Stephen F. Austin, on November 18, 1836 had instructed William H. Wharton, the Texan minister to Washington, to attempt to effect annexation. By union with the United States, Texas would thus have gained American protection against any hostile acts on the part of Mexico.

The United States, however, was troubled by a burgeoning internal controversy over slavery, and the administration of President Andrew Jackson considered Texas a "hot potato" best left alone. Rebuffed, the Texans formally withdrew their offer to join the United States on October 12, 1838.

When Mirabeau B. Lamar succeeded Sam Houston as President of Texas in December 1838, he designed a foreign policy to assure the permanent independence of Texas. To this end President Lamar obtained international recognition of his republic's independence from France (1839), Holland, Belgium, and Great Britain (1840).

In December 1841, however, Sam Houston returned to the presidency and appointed Anson Jones his Secretary of State. Under Houston and Jones, renewed attempts were made to have Texas annexed to the United States. The "accord of the incorporation of Texas into the territory of the United States" to which Foreign Minister José María de Bocanegra was referring was one of these ill-fated attempts by the Houston administration to have Texas join the American Union.

On November 3, 1843 General Juan N. Almonte, the Mexican minister to the United States, reiterated the Mexican threat to declare war against the United States in a letter to Abel P. Upshur, the American Secretary of State.

[1]In Carlos Bosch García (Ed.), *Material para la Historia Diplomática de México y los Estados Unidos, 1820-1848* (Mexico City: Escuela Nacional de Ciencias Politicas y Sociales, 1957), pp. 385-386; hereafter cited as Bosch Garcia, *La Historia Diplomática de México*. See also Manning, *Diplomatic Correspondence of the United States*, VIII, pp. 555-557.

In what can only be described as a "bad neighbor" policy, General Almonte intervened in what he perceived to be American foreign policy toward a third party—Texas. After a diatribe of fantasy against alleged American fomentation of the Texas revolt, Almonte asserted that the United States had earlier recognized the independence of Mexico from Spain. This American recognition, General Almonte continued, had included the recognition of Mexican sovereignty over Texas. The later American recognition of Texan independence from Mexico, General Almonte made it quite clear, was unacceptable to Mexico. Furthermore, the Mexicans felt that their "rights" to Texas "would not be considered diminished" in the slightest by American recognition of Texan independence.

After voicing his hopes that the American Congress would decline to permit the annexation of Texas, General Almonte stated that he had orders to protest as soon as annexation was sanctioned by the American Congress and immediately end his mission in the United States, as Mexico was resolute in its decision to declare war against the United States in the event of American annexation of Texas.[2]

While it is not necessary to rebut each Mexican assertion, General Almonte's statement that the Texan revolution was started by Americans, it should be noted, has already been proven false in previous chapters. General Juan N. Almonte, a long time supporter of Mexico's perennial off-again-on-again president-dictator, General Santa Anna, furthermore, totally neglected to mention his superior's role in provoking the Texan bid for independence and his overthrow of the Mexican federal constitution of 1824. General Almonte also neglected to mention the activity of anti-Santa Anna Mexicans, such as Lorenzo de Zavala, in helping initiate the drive for Texan independence. These facts, however, have been covered in earlier chapters. Further, Mexico's refusal to comply with the Treaty of Velasco in accepting her own recognition of Texan independence, even though Texas fulfilled its part by releasing Santa Anna and the other prisoners, while regretable, is not the major point.

[2]Juan N. Almonte to Abel P. Upshur, Nov. 23, 1843, in Bosch García, *La Historia Diplomática de México*, p. 397.

The important new ingredient, in both the Almonte communication to Secretary of State Upshur and in the earlier Bocanegra communication to the American Minister to Mexico, Waddy Thompson, is the officially declared intention of Mexico to declare war against the United States. Mexico's refusal to accept the fact that the United States had a sovereign right to recognize the independence of Texas and the Mexican disregard for treaties they disliked (*i.e.,* the Treaty of Velasco), simply served as a further warning to this country. After all, an irresponsible nation such as Mexico, which chose to accept only treaties which it fancied (such as the so-called Treaty of Córdoba negotiated with the renegade Spaniard, General Juan O'Donojú) regardless of the legalities of such treaties, while refusing to fulfill its obligations under such bona fide treaties as the Velasco that it found distasteful was indeed a neighbor who needed careful watching.

The Bocanegra and Almonte war threats compounded the dangers that an irresponsible neighbor such as Mexico represented. Next, the position of Mexico in questioning the sovereign right of the United States to recognize the independence of other nations, such as Texas, is anomalous. Finally, once Texas had maintained its independence in the face of Mexican harassment since the inception of the lone star republic's birth, had secured diplomatic recognition from several European governments, along with American diplomatic recognition, and in addition had a peace treaty with Mexico—however Mexico may have subsequently chosen to disregard this treaty—the actions of Mexico are both incomprehensible and reprehensible.

In addition, the ruling class of Mexico and almost all her top officials were military men. In view of the above facts, any nation that would threaten war against a neighbor with which it had never hitherto been at war, and against which it thus lacked an historic desire for revenge, like France and Germany, must certainly be led by men who loved war and bloodshed for its own sake.

The unnecessary butcheries perpetrated by the Mexicans under Santa Anna's command at San Patricio, el Refugio,

Goliad, and Guadalupe Victoria, which were so deplored by the Italian-born and naturalized Mexican, General Vicente Filisola, who succeeded Santa Anna as general-in-chief of the Mexican forces to conquer Texas after the latter's defeat and capture at San Jacinto, have already been noted. The murderous slaughter perpetrated by the Mexicans at the Alamo is so well known as to need no further discussion. Perhaps this bloodthirsty activity of the Mexicans is a throwback to their Aztec ancestors who had practiced human sacrifice to their serpent-war god, Quetzalcoatle! Santa Anna at the Alamo and his military successors in the presidential palace, which was built on the ruins of Tenochtitlán, might indeed have fancied themselves as latter-day Montezumas offering gringo blood to their war god.

That Mexico had no legal grounds on which to dictate to foreign nations as to whether they could recognize each other, form alliances, or be united one to the other, goes without saying. That Mexico chose to dictate American foreign policy regarding Texas and back her dictum with threats of war was a warning that no American president could afford to ignore. If and when the United States and Texas agreed to annexation, the President of the United States at that time would have to take precautionary and defensive steps in preparation for the war that Mexico had threatened. The fact that a potential enemy may be both militarily weak and somewhat mad is no reason to ignore his war threats.

In the event that Texas were annexed to the United States, any American president who chose to disregard Mexico's war threats would be failing in his constitutional duty to protect the American people from the threat of foreign invasion. Such a president would indeed be guilty of a high crime and be giving a declared potential enemy aid and comfort. On the other hand, whatever actions such an American president might take to anticipate, thwart, or weaken Mexico would be wholly in line with his duty to protect the United States. Finally, it should be understood that while Mexico's military power might appear puny against the United States in the 20th century, it was quantitatively quite respectable vis-à-vis the American army just prior to the Mexican War. In fact, when that war did break out, the United States was at a decided numerical disadvantage. The determining factor, as things turned out, was the superior fighting ability of the American soldiers, and their ability to handle heavy guns.

The two aforementioned Mexican war threats, however unprovoked on the part of the United States, were merely the beginning. On April 22, 1844 General Juan N. Almonte, still the Mexican Minister to the United States, wrote to the new American Secretary of State, John C. Calhoun. Former Secretary Upshur had been killed in an explosion aboard the American ship *Princeton,* and John C. Calhoun had succeeded him in the State Department. To make sure that the American government, and the new Secretary of State in particular, held no illusions regarding the Mexican war threats of August 23 and November 3, 1843, General Almonte affirmed in his letter to Calhoun that those declarations were still in effect.

The United States, in the meantime, had negotiated a treaty of annexation with the Republic of Texas. The American government, under the administration of President John Tyler, while declining to have American foreign policy formulated by the current clique of generals in control of Mexico City, nonetheless—and in view of the obvious interest the Mexicans had displayed on the subject of the possible American annexation of Texas—as a matter of diplomatic courtesy kept the Mexican government informed regarding the pending union.

On May 23, 1844, Benjamin E. Green, American chargé d'affaires ad interim in Mexico City and the son of the famous Duff Green, wrote to the Mexican Minister of Foreign Relations, José María de Bocanegra. In the spirit of peace and good neighborliness, Green informed Bocanegra that a treaty for the annexation of Texas to the United States had been signed by the plenipotentiaries of both republics. This treaty, furthermore, would shortly be submitted to the United States Senate for ratification.

The American chargé d'affaires, in the most diplomatic language, which contrasted sharply with bellicose Mexican communications on this subject, told Foreign Minister Bocanegra that the United States was being forced to annex Texas in order to prevent the latter from falling under the influence of Great Britain.

Ever since the British had abolished slavery throughout their own empire in 1833, they had sought to encourage other governments to do likewise. In view of this and in view of the strategic location of Texas in the event of another Anglo-American war, the United States was reluctant to see Texas fall under British influence. An abolitionist Texas, offering a haven to runaway American slaves and perhaps even fomenting a slave insurrection in Louisiana and adjacent American states with British support and encouragement, would be intolerable. In addition, a Texas that permitted Great Britain to station troops and extended other facilities to a British army intent upon invading the United States represented a clear threat to the latter's security. Texas, for its part, was determined to resist any and all future Mexican invasions. To do so more effectively, it was desirable either to join the United States or become aligned with Great Britain.

In writing to Foreign Minister Bocanegra, the American chargé d'affaires hoped the Mexican would understand that no ill intent toward Mexico was envisaged.

Green's friendly and diplomatic letter was answered exactly one week later on May 30, 1844. In his reply, Foreign Minister Bocanegra repeated the old Mexican clichés about Texan "colonists" usurping the territory of Texas with the aid of the United States. Bocanegra also affirmed the Mexican intention "to repossess herself of Texas" and attacked American diplomiatic recognition "of the independence of Texas, as an act aggressive to her [Mexico's] sovereignty."[3] For some unexplainable reason Bocanegra failed to draw the parallel that the earlier diplomatic recognition of Mexican independence by the United States was in any way an aggressive act against Spain.

More importantly, Bocanegra refused to consider a treaty of limits with the United States, informing Chargé d'Affaires Green that he had "express orders from the President of the

[3] In Manning, *Diplomatic Correspondence of the United States*, VIII, p. 589. Also see Bosch Garcia, *La Historia Diplomática de México*, pp. 424-425.

Republic [of Mexico] to say and affirm in the most conclusive and express manner, that Mexico had not renounced, nor should not renounce, nor in any manner cedes the totality or part of her rights" to Texas.[4] Ironically, the Mexican President of the Republic to whom Bocanegra referred, was the same General Antonio López de Santa Anna who had concluded the Treaty of Velasco recognizing the independence of the Republic of Texas in 1836! Santa Anna, it should be noted, was to slide in and out of the presidential palace as through a revolving door for a generation. This current presidential term began in 1843 with the promulgation of a new constitution giving Santa Anna dictatorial powers and ended in 1844 when a revolution overthrew the dictator.

On a more ominous note, Foreign Minister Bocanegra mentioned his earlier communication to Waddy Thompson, former American Minister to Mexico, stating its exact date, August 23, 1843, and specifically quoted his own threat "that Mexico will consider as a declaration of War against the Mexican Republic, the ratification of that agreement for the incorporation of Texas into the territory of the United States." Bocanegra concluded his letter by reaffirming this threat to declare war against the United States in the event that the annexation treaty should be approved by the United States Senate.[5]

Chargé d'Affaires Green answered Foreign Minister Bocanegra the next day in a polite but firm letter that clearly exposed the Mexican "claim" to Texas as the claptrap it was. Green stated bluntly:

> The Govt of the U.S. . . . neither directly nor indirectly, admits that Mexico is the legal proprietor of Texas, or that any apology or explanation is due her, as such.
>
> The independence of Texas having been recognized, not only by the U.S., but by all the other principal powers of the world, most of whom have established diplomatic relations with her, she is to be regarded as an independent and sovereign power, competent to treat for herself; and as she had shaken off the authority of Mexico, and successfully resisted her power for

[4]May 30, 1844, in Manning, *Diplomatic Correspondence of the United States*, VIII, p. 591.
[5]*Ibid.*

eight years, the U.S. are under no obligation to respect her former relations with this country [Mexico].

The Govt of the U.S. however, has thought proper, in a friendly and candid manner, to explain to Mexico the motives of its conduct; & this it has thought due to Mexico, not as the proprietor of Texas, either de jure or de facto, but as a mutual neighbor of Texas & the U.S., and one of the family of American Republics.

The undersigned [Green] must be allowed here to express his surprise, that Mexico should renew her unfounded protests against the course, which the Govt of the U.S. has thought proper to adopt, in relation to the Republic of Texas; and more especially, that she should address those protests to that community of nations, which by recognizing the independence of Texas, have long since denied to Mexico any right to complain.

The American chargé d'affaires ad interim at Mexico City then made a most telling comment. Benjamin E. Green stated:

The ground assumed by H.E. [His Excellency, *i.e.*, Mexican Foreign Minister José María de Bocanegra] that Mexico by futile protests upon paper, could retain her rights over the territory of Texas, notwithstanding the facts, which are notorious, that Texas has declared and maintained her independence for a long space of years, that during that length of time Mexico has been unable to reconquer her, and has of late ceased all efforts to do so, is truly novel and extraordinary. As well might Mexico, by similar protests, declare that the world is her empire, and the various nations, who people it, her subjects; and expect her claim to be recognized.[6]

Green then went on to express his regret that Mexico had rejected the friendly proposals of the American government to settle "by amicable negotiations" whatever questions might grow out of current Mexican-American relations and stated "that if war does ensue, as threatened by Mexico, Mexico herself will be the aggressor, and will alone be responsible for all the evils, which may attend it."[7]

[6]May 31, 1844, *ibid.*, p. 594.
[7]*Ibid.*

On June 7, 1844 Benjamin E. Green dispatched a letter to Secretary of State John C. Calhoun. Keeping Calhoun posted on the latest Mexican developments relating to Texas, Green informed the Secretary of State that the Mexican Congress had met for the purpose of increasing their army in order to provide the means to invade and conquer Texas. The chargé d'affaires then opined that the Mexican president, General Antonio López de Santa Anna, would not be able to send another army to Texas. Green felt that General Santa Anna would "not trust his valuable person there again, and he will be very loth to send another general to do that, in which he failed." Furthermore, Green pointed out, Santa Anna lacked the funds to raise the necessary army. On the other hand, Green informed Calhoun that General Santa Anna had proposed to "disencumber" the Mexican clergy of $4,000,000 for the war effort and to raise 30,000 troops.[8]

From Green's letter to Calhoun it is apparent that, however unsuccessful the outcome was likely to be, there did exist a Mexican desire for war. Foolish military adventures, with slight chance of success at best, have been undertaken both before and after the Mexican War.

Forewarned of Mexico's hostile intentions by both General Juan N. Almonte, the Mexican minister to the United States, and José María de Bocanegra, the Mexican Foreign Minister, and now apprised by Chargé d'Affaires Benjamin E. Green of the Mexican president's warlike intentions, the United States necessarily accepted the possibility of a Mexican attack. In the event that Texas did join the United States, a Mexican attack on Texas would of course be an attack on the United States itself.

In a letter to Green dated June 12, 1844, Foreign Minister Bocanegra claimed that, by entering into a treaty of annexation with Texas, the United States was violating the Mexican-American treaty of December 1, 1832. This treaty dealt with amity, commerce, navigation, and boundaries. Bocanegra's point, apparently, was that the United States, having once signed such a treaty with Mexico, was forever frozen in its relations with

[8]*Ibid.*, p. 601.

that country, despite internal Mexican fragmentation and border alterations growing out of Mexican struggles with her own federal states. The fact that Texas had maintained its independence for eight years in the face of Mexican hostility and had received international recognition of its independence Bocanegra failed to acknowledge. Bocanegra also failed to contend, as long as he was assuming such an ultra-legalistic approach, that the United States had been wrong in dealing with the Mexicans prior to December 28, 1836. It was on the latter date that the Spanish government of Queen Isabel II deigned to recognize the independent status of the Mexican rebels in what had hitherto formed a part of the Viceroyalty of New Spain.[9]

How the Mexicans could keep insisting, apparently with a straight face, that it was quite proper for the United States to violate its relations with Spain by treating with the Mexicans before the latter had received Spanish recognition, but improper for the United States to treat Texas as an independent state, can perhaps best be answered by a student of international law whose major is psychiatry!

That the United States continued to humor these Mexican fantasies, to the extent of maintaining diplomatic correspondence with such misguided officials as Bocanegra and Almonte, is a tribute to American willingness to bend over backward to avoid war. To have gone the additional mile and have permitted American foreign policy to be set in Mexico City would have been a surrender of American sovereignty.

The Mexican authorities, for their part, were either blind to the inconsistency of their argument or else were determined to get their own way by whatever means. Furthermore, use of an "outside enemy" did serve to distract the Mexican people from their own internal problems, thus providing the Mexican military some advantage as the generals attempted to maintain their control over that wretched land. Also, under the guise of a war issue, the church could be divested of its property, to the enrichment of the generals!

Foreign Minister Bocanegra, in his June 12, 1844 letter to

[9]Toro, *Compendio de Historia de México*, p. 336.

American Chargé d'Affaires Green, went yet another step toward the ridiculous. In that letter the Mexican Foreign Minister admitted that Great Britain and France had indeed recognized the independence of Texas. However, while admitting the obvious, Bocanegra made his admission a begrudging one by stating "that if these two Great nations did lend themselves to this acknowledgement of Independence they did so . . . by acknowledging a fact, and nothing more."[10]

So now it was quite correct for Great Britain and France to acknowledge the "fact" of Texan independence. Only the United States of America should be denied that same sovereign right to acknowledge the "fact" of the independence of the Republic of Texas! There is no mention in this letter of Great Britain or France being in any way unkind to Mexico, let alone violating their prior recognition of Mexico or Mexican sovereignty. Bocanegra, in fact, goes to the incredible extent of becoming an advocate for the British and French right to recognize Texan independence! In this regard, His Excellency don José María de Bocanegra informed the American chargé d'affaires:

> . . . France and England have on various occasions, interposed their high respect and worthy influence, to procure a cessation of the [Mexican-Texan] war; never however have they termed it unjust, but only injurious and pernicious, from its very nature.
>
> Nor could such great powers have acted in any other way in acknowledging that in a country independent in fact [Texas], but depending in right upon a mother country [Mexico], the fact alone, and not the right can be acknowledged. . . . [11]

This incredible Mexican defense of the British and French right to acknowledge Texan independence, while denying that same right to the United States, is the type of "reasoning" that ultimately led to the Mexican War. The entire Mexican psychology on the subject of Texas might best be described as an Alice in Wonderland logic.

[10]In Manning, *Diplomatic Correspondence of the United States*, VIII, p. 610; Bosch García, *La Historia Diplomática de México*, p. 430.

[11]In Manning, *Diplomatic Correspondence of the United States*, VIII, p. 611.

Very simply, Texas either was independent in fact or it was not. Texas could hardly be independent for British and French purposes, but somehow not quite independent for American purposes.

Before concluding with Bocanegra's incredible letter, it is only fair to mention that the Mexican Foreign Minister was at least consistent in his inconsistency. Bocanegra did indeed take umbrage that the United States had concluded "a treaty with the so-called Republic of Texas."

Mexico, of course, was well aware that Texas was independent. As already stated, Foreign Minister Bocanegra admitted this when he accepted the British and French acknowledgment of the "fact" of independence. Also, General José María Tornel y Mendivil, Mexico's off-again-on-again Minister of War, admitted that Texas was lost to Mexico.[12] Much earlier, as previously mentioned, General Vicente Filisola had also admitted that Texas was lost to Mexico forever.[13]

[12]Green to Calhoun, June 7, 1844, *ibid.*, p. 601.
[13]Filisola, *Memoria de la Guerra de Tejas*, p. 132.

8
Reports from Mexico

On June 8, 1844 the treaty to annex Texas to the United States—over which Mexican Foreign Minister José Maria de Bocanegra, and the Mexican minister to the United States, General Juan N. Almonte, had threatened war—was rejected by the United States Senate by a vote of 35-16.

The defeat of the annexation treaty did not end the Texas question. On June 17, Chargé d'Affaires Benjamin E. Green in Mexico City wrote Secretary of State John C. Calhoun regarding British influence. The American chargé informed the secretary that the President of Mexico, General Santa Anna, would rather see Texas in the hands of Great Britain than in those of the United States. Green explained that the reason for this was that the English merchants in Mexico all favored Santa Anna's government. This English support, Green continued, was because of the fact that under Santa Anna "*negocios* [which in English may be rendered *transactions* effected by bribery] are most frequent and most profitable."[1]

Chargé d'Affairs Green went on to state that the British were Santa Anna's best customers. They paid most liberally for exclu-

[1]In Manning, *Diplomatic Correspondence of the United States*, VIII, 615; Bosch García, *La Historia Diplomática de México*, p. 432.

sive import licenses. While the English made money, Santa Anna also profited, amassing golden ounces. Thus the English and Santa Anna both served each other, and the interest of Great Britain was on Santa Anna's side. To show the importance of these Anglo-*santannista* transactions, Green stated that the Mexican Minister of the Treasury made over $100,000 in three months by means of such "*negocios*."[1] It should be understood that the $100,000 referred to was in dollars of the year 1844. In view of inflation for well over a century and a quarter (despite periods of temporary depression), the purchasing power of $100,000 in 1844 was far greater than today. In Bosch García, who gives a synopsis of the letter, the $100,000 is rendered "a million pesos."

Benjamin E. Green further said that Santa Anna, naturally leaned to the English interest. At the same time, the Mexican president hated the United States government and people. Unable to forget or forgive his disgrace and defeat at San Jacinto, Santa Anna preferred to see Great Britain encircle the United States "on every side, and strangle our growing commerce and power in her strong embrace."[2]

Informing Secretary of State Calhoun that Santa Anna was "making preparations to invade Texas with a large force," Green observed that only a few months previous the Mexican War Minister, General José María Tornel y Mendívil, had acknowledged to then United States Minister Thompson that it was impossible for Mexico to reconquer Texas. In support of the Tornel statement, Green enclosed an extract of a letter from Thompson to himself, dated March 27, 1844. In the extract, Thompson quotes General Tornel as saying: "Texas is gone forever from Mexico. All we desire is to save the '*decoro nacional*' [national honor]."[3]

In a memorandum enclosed with the extract Thompson wrote:

> Here is an acknowledgement that Mexico is unable to enforce the right, which she asserts, to reconquer Texas. The

[2]*Ibid.*
[3]*Ibid.*; also see Bosch García, June 7, 1844, *La Historia Diplomática de México*, 429.

person, who makes it, is one of the Cabinet, the Minister of War [General José María Tornel y Mendívil], who ought to be best informed on the subject of Mexico's military abilities. At the time it was made, he was universally admitted to be the best informed and ablest of the Cabinet, of which he was a leading spirit, & whose sentiments he spoke.

How long then are other nations to wait upon the "decoro nacional" of Mexico? Certainly not longer than their own safety & interests permit.[4]

After thus quoting Thompson and, indirectly General Tornel, Green stated that Tornel undoubtedly spoke Santa Anna's sentiments. Furthermore, Green asserted, these were "the sentiments of the most intelligent men, in and out of Mexico." The conquest of Texas being thus ruled out, Green questioned Santa Anna's motives in preparing an expedition and sending troops secretly to the frontier. Green wrote:

Is it the mere thirst for blood? Is it that he [Santa Anna] merely seeks to ravage the country, to surprise, kill and make prisoners, and then retire, after the manner of Genl [Adrian] Woll, from [San Antonio de] Bejar?[5]

Chargé d'Affaires Green next mentioned that the Mexicans had sent a special messenger to England in the last Havana packet. The purpose of the messenger, Green stated, was rumored to be an offer to sell Texas to England. Green continued:

This I could not for a moment believe; for besides, that Mexico, not being in possession of Texas, could not sell, England, having acknowledged the independence of Texas could not buy of Mexico. I have since however been led to believe (chiefly from the change of feeling towards Texas in the British legation here) that there may be some truth in what I supposed at first to be the most ridiculous of rumours.

Mexico has rejected the opportunity of settling this Texas war, from which the Mexican Govt itself has no hopes of a

[4]In Manning, *Diplomatic History of the United States*, VIII, p. 616.
[5]*Ibid.*

favourable conclusion. . . . Why then does he [Santa Anna] persist? Will a sanguinary and vindictive spirit account for it, fully & satisfactorily? It might perhaps, were it not that the feelings of the English Legation here have wonderfully changed of late, as regards Texas. From being her warm friends and the advocates of her independence, they now *damn* the Texans, and the British Minister says, that his Govt committed a great mistake in ever recognizing their independence. Why? *Because as yet they had gained nothing by it.*

It may then be that Santa Anna expects, by a rapid movement with a large army, to overrun Texas; & hold it some 60 or 90 days; & then by a hasty transfer, sell it to England, before the Texans shall be able to rally and drive him back.[6]

On July 2, 1844, Mexican Foreign Minister José María de Bocanegra, in a letter to the American chargé d'affaires, again repeated his earlier war threat. Bocanegra informed Green that Mexico would "justly regard, as equivalent to a declaration of war, the annexation of Texas to the United States."[7]

In the following month the United States received still further warning of hostile Mexican intentions. On August 18, 1844 the United States consul at Monterey, California, Thomas O. Larkin, wrote to Secretary of State John C. Calhoun. The latter was informed that the Mexican military governor of California, General Manuel Micheltorena, had "received orders to place every port of California in the best state of defence . . . as the Mexican Government expect that the U.S. Senate would annex Texas to the Union, in which case Gen. Santa Anna would immediately declare war." Larkin further informed Secretary of State Calhoun that England might purchase California from Mexico.[8]

Benjamin E. Green, writing to Calhoun from Mexico City on August 20, 1844, informed the Secretary of State that "Since the arrival of the last packet from England, the movement against Texas has been pushed with fresh vigor." Green further stated that the original Mexican plan to invade Texas by land had been

[6]*Ibid.*
[7]*Ibid.*, p. 627.
[8]*Ibid.*, pp. 638-639.

abandoned in favor of a sea attack. The Mexican plan called for burning Galveston to the ground,

> . . . and the war is to be one of extermination. The soil [of Texas] is to be purged of every drop of Anglo-Saxon blood. The decree of the 17th July 1843,—the same, which legalized the massacres of Tabasco—is to be enforced in the same way in Texas, as soon as the Mexican Army shall have gained possession!![9]

Green also informed Secretary of State Calhoun that he had received a letter from the United States consul at Tabasco, Mexico, a Mr. E. Porter, regarding the incarceration of several American citizens. Tabasco, incidentally, is located on the Gulf of Mexico, between the Isthmus of Tehuantepec and Guatemala. Apparently the former governor of Tabasco, General Francisco Sentmanat, had attempted some military action with a small band of followers, including a few Americans. Green enclosed a copy of Porter's letter, along with his own letter to the secretary of state. The Porter letter read in part:

> Sentmanat and his men succeeded in landing, & passed through the woods up the country, where they surrendered to the govt troops, on the promise of being pardoned by their laying down their arms; Ex-Govr. Sentmanat being the only person that fired a shot on the occasion. He was taken prisoner, and shot; his head cut off, fried in boiling oil, put on a spike, hung up in an iron cage, & exhibited in the public square for days.

Porter also informed Green in this same letter that the entire party had been put to death. Furthermore, the current governor of Tabasco, General Pedro de Ampudia, "was hostile to all and everything American."[10]

The importance of this letter lies in the fact that it confirms the bloodthirstiness of General Pedro de Ampudia and that it

[9]*Ibid.*, p. 639.
[10]Letter of July 20, 1844, *ibid.*, pp. 639-640.

also exposes General Ampudia's strong hostility against the United States. General Pedro de Ampudia was later to play an important role in bringing about the Mexican War. The specific activities of General Ampudia in helping to provoke the Mexican War will be dealt with in Chapter 12.

On October 14, 1844, in what was to form a part of the famous Shannon-Rejón Correspondence, Wilson Shannon, newly appointed United States minister to Mexico, wrote to Manuel Crescencio Rejón, Mexico's new Minister of Foreign Relations. Shannon informed Rejón that the President of the United States, John Tyler, had learned with deep regret about the Mexican determination to renew the war against the Republic of Texas. Furthermore, Shannon stated that he had been instructed by the President to protest both against the proposed Mexican invasion and the manner in which it was to be conducted. Shannon mentioned Santa Anna's decree of June 17, 1843, under which General Francisco Sentmanat (mentioned in the Porter-Green Correspondence) and his party had been executed. As General Adrian Woll, who was to lead the Mexican invasion of Texas, intended to carry out the decree of June 17, 1843, a war of extermination would result. Shannon, furthermore, objected to the "barbarous mode, in which the Government of Mexico has proclaimed to the world her intention to conduct the war."

Shannon next inquired as to the Mexican object of renewing the war with Texas at that particular time, pointing out that the Mexican-Texas War had been virtually suspended for eight years. Answering his own rhetorical question, Shannon stated:

> But one object can be assigned, and that is to defeat the annexation of Texas to the United States. She [Mexico] knows full well that the measure [the annexation of Texas to the United States] is still pending, and that the rejection of the Treaty has but postponed it. She [Mexico] knows that, when Congress adjourned, it was pending in both Houses, ready to be taken up and acted upon at its next meeting, and that it is at present activity canvassed by the people throughout the union. She [Mexico] is not ignorant that the decision will, in all probability

be in its favour, unless it should be defeated by some movement exterior to the United States. The projected invasion of Texas by Mexico, at this time, is that movement, and is intended to effect it, either by conquering and subjugating Texas to her power, or by forcing her to withdraw her proposition for annexation and to form other connections less acceptable to her.

Shannon then bluntly told Mexican Foreign Minister Rejón:

> The United States can not, while the measure of annexation is pending, stand quietly by and permit either of these results. It has been a measure of policy long cherished and deemed indispensable to their safety and welfare, and has accordingly been an object steadily pursued by all parties, and the acquisition of the territory made the subject of negociation [sic] by almost every administration for the last twenty years. This policy may be traced to the belief, generally entertained, that Texas was embraced in the cession of Louisiana by France to the United States in 1803, and was improperly surrendered by the Treaty of Florida in 1819; connected with the fact that a large portion of the Territory lies in the valley of the Mississippi and is indispensable to the defence of a distant, and important frontier. The hazard of a conflict of policy upon important points between the United States and one of the leading European Powers, since the recognition of Texas, has rendered the acquisition still more essential to their safety and welfare, and, accordingly, has increased in proportion the necessity of acquiring it. . . .
>
> The President . . . would accordingly be compelled to regard the invasion of Texas by Mexico, while the question of annexation is pending, as highly offensive to the United States.[11]

Shannon next informed Rejón that President Tyler entertained no doubt as to the right of the United States to invite Texas to renew the proposition for annexation. Moreover,

---

[11]*Ibid.*, pp. 645-647; Bosch García, *La Historia Diplomática de México*, p. 447. While a confusion of dates exists between Green (*July* 17, 1843) and Shannon (*June* 17, 1843), they were both talking about the same decree.

Texas, as an independent state, had a right to accept the invitation without consulting Mexico. The American minister continued to inform Rejón that President Tyler regarded Texas, in every respect, as independent of Mexico and as competent to transfer the whole or part of her territory to the United States.

Shannon then offered a brief review of Mexican history, explaining that Santa Anna had subverted the Mexican federal constitution of 1824. Of the several states of the Mexican confederation that had resisted Santa Anna's usurpation, only Texas had been able to maintain its freedom from the dictator. Texas had stood up to Santa Anna in defense of her rights and independence, had successfully asserted them on the battleground of San Jacinto in 1836, and had ever since maintained them.

Once again Shannon told Rejón that the United States would not permit annexation to be defeated by an invasion of Texas while annexation was pending. Shannon then took exception to the Mexican view that the Texans were

> . . . lawless intruders and usurpers, without political existence, who may be rightfully treated as a gang of pirates and outcasts from society, and, as such, not entitled to the protection of the laws of nations or humanity. In this assumption the Government of Mexico obstinately persists, in spite of the well known fact, universally admitted by all except itself, that the colonists, who settled Texas, instead of being intruders and usurpers, were invited to settle there, first, under a grant by the Spanish authority to Moses Austin, which was afterwards confirmed by the Mexican authority, and, afterwards, by similar grants from the state of Coahuila and Texas, which it was authorized to make by the Constitution of 1824. They came there then as invited guests, not invited for their own interests, but for those of Spain and Mexico, in order to protect a weak and helpless province from wandering tribes of Indians; to improve, cultivate and render productive wild and almost uninhabited wastes, and to make that valuable, which was before worthless. All this they effected at great cost and much danger and difficulty, which nothing but american [sic] energy, industry and perseverance could have overcome; not only unaided by Mex-

ico, but in despite of the impediments caused by her interference.[12]

In his concluding statements Wilson Shannon made known to Foreign Minister Rejón the view of the United States Government regarding the Texans:

Instead then of a lawless band of adventurers, as they are assumed to be by the Government of Mexico, these invited [Texans] colonists became in a few years constituent portions of one of the members of the Mexican Federation, and since their separation have established wise and free institutions, under the influence of which they have enjoyed peace and security, while their energy and industry, protected by equal laws, have widely extended the limits of cultivation and improvement. It is such a people, living under such institutions, successfully resisting all attacks from the period of their separation nine years ago, and who have been recognized and admitted into the family of nations, that Mexico has undertaken to regard as lawless banditti, and against whom, as such, she has proclaimed a war of extermination, forgetful of their exalted and generous humanity in refusing to exercise the just rights of retaliation, when, in a former invasion, victory placed in their hands the most ample means of doing so. The Government of Mexico may delude itself by its fictions; but it cannot delude the rest of the world. It will be held responsible, not by what it may choose to regard as facts, but what are in reality such, and known and acknowledged, so to be, by all save itself.

Such are the views entertained by the President of the United States, in regard to the proposed invasion, while the question of annexation is pending, and of the barbarous and bloodly manner, in which, it is proclaimed, it will be conducted; and in conformity to his instructions, the undersigned hereby solemnly protests against both, as highly injurious and offensive to the United States.[13]

In a letter to Secretary of State Calhoun, dated October 28, 1844, Wilson Shannon made it clear that Mexico was determined

[12]In Manning, *Diplomatic Correspondence of the United States*, VIII, pp. 648-649.
[13]*Ibid.*, p. 649.

to renew the war against Texas. Shannon explained that the Mexicans supposed that, by renewing hostilities against Texas, they would either subjugate the latter republic "or force her into an alliance with England, under a guarantee from that power that she should in no event transfer her sovereignty to the U. States."

Informing the Secretary further of Mexico's hostile attitude against the United States, Shannon stated that it had been the policy of all parties in Mexico to represent the United States "as a dangerous and grasping neighbor, and that it was necessary for the safety of Mexico we should be held at a distance." On this basis Shannon explained the hostility of the Santa Anna government and the Mexican people against the annexation of Texas to the United States. Shannon further stated that this hatred was the cause of the Mexican policy, "which has been adopted and adhered to for years past, in utter disregard of all treaty stipulations, of preventing, by every possible means, our citizens from settling in Mexico . . . and also of driving those out of the country, who are located in it."

Thus, despite the fact that the Mexican War Minister, General Tornel y Mendívil, had earlier acknowledged the impossibility of a Mexican conquest of Texas, Shannon gauged that Mexico would attempt the futile task. That Mexico was planning to attack Texas, Shannon left no doubt, informing Calhoun as to the Mexican war plans:

> The plan of the [Mexican] campaign is said to be to concentrate about ten thousand troops at Vera Cruz & convey them direct from that place, by means of transports and steam vessels, to Galveston, with the view of taking that City, & overrunning Eastern Texas; while the army under Genl [Adrian] Woll is to be strengthened, cross the Rio Grande, and invade Texas on the west and form a junction with the Eastern division of the army at some central point. In view of this plan of attack, Mexico sent her two steamers to New York to be repaired, and contracted for four additional ones, with some small crafts.[14]

[14]*Ibid.*, 650-651; Bosch García, *La Historia Diplomática de México*, p. 448.

Shannon also mentioned that Mexico had negotiated a contract for the construction of several vessels in England. The Mexicans, however, did not at that time attack Texas. The explanation for Mexico's failure to strike in 1844 appears later in this informative letter where Shannon states that the opposition to President Santa Anna, centered in the Mexican Congress, was afraid to place too large a military force in Santa Anna's hands. Shannon continues:

> In this state of party strife here [in Mexico City], with the known views of the President of the U.S. [John Tyler]; in relation to a renewal of the war against Texas, I feel confident that that measure will be abandoned at least for the present; that the two parties will come to an open rupture, and that a revolution [against Santa Anna], to say the least, is probable.

Shannon made it quite clear, however, that both President Santa Anna and his opponents were "united on this question [war against Texas], and each appear to be zealously in favor of a vigorous prosecution of the war.[15] The Mexican intention to invade Texas, it may be pointed out, was abandoned temporarily because of party strife and not by reason of any change of heart. It may also be stated that Mexico contemplated such an invasion despite the known determination of President John Tyler to defend Texas. On April 11, 1844 Secretary of State Calhoun had written to Issac Van Zandt and James Pinckney Henderson, the Texan minister-negotiators in Washington, pledging on the President's behalf to defend Texas against a Mexican invasion pending ratification of the annexation treaty. Calhoun had specifically told the Texans:

> . . . I am directed by the President to say that the Sec'y of the Navy has been instructed to order a strong naval force to concentrate in the Gulf of Mexico, to meet any emergency, and that similar orders have been issued by the Secretary of War to moove [sic] the disposable military forces on our Southwestern frontier for the same purpose. . . . I am further directed by the

[15]*Ibid.*

President to say that, during the pendency of the treaty of annexation, he would deem it his duty to use all the means placed within his power by the constitution to protect Texas from all foreign invasion.[16]

As Shannon pointed out, President Tyler's views were known to the Mexicans. Furthermore, in spite of the technicality that the annexation treaty had failed, the United States—having invited Texas to request annexation and having promised protection pending ratification of the treaty—could hardly abandon Texas without loss of national honor. As events were to prove, the United States had not given up on annexation. The point made here is quite simple: Mexico, with full knowledge of probable American military involvement on behalf of Texas, was prepared to invade that republic. Mexico thus courted a Mexican-American war as early as 1844. These Mexican war plans were momentarily shelved, as Minister Shannon had prophesied, by an internal revolution that ousted President Santa Anna.

Shannon's concluding remarks to Secretary of State Calhoun are worth repeating:

> That a feeling of hostility should exist against us with this [Mexican] people is by no means strange, when we recollect that for years past opposition to the U.S. has been used by both parties as a lever by which to obtain public favour and political power. We have been represented as seeking to overrun all Mexico, and that, if not held in check, we would plant the American standard on the walls of the Capitol [of Mexico]. Such has been the unjust and odious light, in which we have been held up to this people by the political men of all parties, until they have created a public opinion, which they cannot, if they were so disposed, easily resist or control. It is true that many intelligent Mexicans privately entertain & express opinions favourable to the amicable arrangement of the difficulties with Texas, & believe that the proposed invasion, if attempted, would result in no good to Mexico. But there are few, who have the boldness to

[16]In the Anson Jones Papers, Barker History Center, University of Texas, Austin, Texas.

express these opinions publicly, or who would be willing to stem the current of popular prejudice by undertaking to carry them out. I am not aware that these opinions prevail to any extent in the army, which is the great controlling power in the country. I think we must therefore rely on time and a new combination of circumstances to dissipate these prejudices against us, before we can reasonably hope to acquire by negociation [sic] any portion of the territory now claimed by Mexico, and I do not think we have any grounds to flatter ourselves that a favourable change in this respect will soon take place. . . .[17]

On October 31, 1844 the Mexican Minister of Foreign Relations, Manuel Rejón, wrote to Minister Shannon. A translation of this letter can be found in William R. Manning's *Diplomatic Correspondence of the United States,* VIII. To his credit, Rejón admitted that the first Texan colonists had established themselves in that territory by concessions of the Spanish Government, thus antedating the establishment of an independent Mexico. Rejón further admitted that these concessions were subsequently confirmed by the newly independent Mexican Government. In addition, he acknowledged that later concessions were "granted by the state of Coahuila and Texas, duly authorized to grant them."

Rejón's complaint thus narrowed to the fact that the principal figures in the movement for Texan independence were "almost all natives of the United States."[18] Rejón also objected to the fact that individual Americans had aided the Texan forces against Santa Anna. Rejón felt, and not without just cause, that many of these Americans were motivated to aid Texas in the hope of annexing it ultimately to the United States. Rejón would have preferred that the United States Government had intervened, *on behalf of Santa Anna,* to thwart individual American volunteers from aiding Texas. The United States, having failed to check the flow of volunteer American fighting men and munitions to Texas, was thus indicted by the Mexican Foreign Minister for complicity in the establishment of an independent

[17]Oct. 28, 1844, in Manning, *Diplomatic Correspondence of the United States,* VIII, p. 653.
[18]*Ibid.,* p. 654.

Republic of Texas. To accuse the United States of complicity in the Texan war of independence because it failed to intervene *on behalf of Santa Anna,* is, in this author's opinion, stretching things a bit too far. The fact is that it is quite doubtful, even assuming that President Andrew Jackson in 1836 had wished to help Santa Anna, that the United States could effectively have prevented individual Americans from coming to the assistance of the beleaguered Texans.

Foreign Minister Rejón again returned to his basic theme that the Texans who proclaimed the independence of Texas were emigrants from the United States. Somewhere in his argument against the American "emigrants," Rejón lost sight of the fact that the very Texans who were instrumental in proclaiming the independence of Texas were by that time naturalized Mexican citizens! Throwing the entire blame for the independence of Texas on the native-born Americans, he failed even to mention the names of Lorenzo de Zavala and other native Spanish-speaking and Mexican-born Mexicans who were in the forefront of the Texan revolt.

As regards Santa Anna's destruction of the Mexican federation in 1835 by his overthrow of the Mexican federal constitution of 1824, Rejón glossed over this point. He was unfortunately blind to the fact that the Texan war for independence was simply an extension of the Mexican civil war that President Santa Anna himself inaugurated when he overthrew the federal government of Mexico in order to establish his own dictatorship.

Perhaps with injured Mexican pride, Rejón could not see that the largely American-born army of Texas was superior to that of the Mexicans. Whereas Santa Anna had crushed the *federalista* opposition elsewhere in Mexico, he was unable to establish his authority in Texas, the one remaining segment of the old Mexican federation as established by the constitution of 1824.

Unable to evict Santa Anna from all Mexico and re-establish the old federal government, the Texan *federalistas* were forced on the defensive against the usurper. They were able to maintain their rights, as guaranteed in the Mexican federal constitution of 1824, only in Texas itself. Inevitably, such a stalemate—with

Santa Anna controlling the rest of Mexico and the Texan *federalistas* controlling only Texas—led to the independence of the latter. To Foreign Minister Rejón, however, Santa Anna's usurpation of power was merely a "pretext" for the Texans. Even assuming for a moment Rejón's point of view, freedom from an arbitrary military dictatorship is an excellent pretext for revolt!

Rejón next addressed himself to the belief held by a number of Americans that Texas had been part of the Louisiana Purchase. In repudiating any American claim to Texas based on that belief, he came out strongly in favor of the sanctity of treaties, indignantly writing:

> . . . taking up now that belief, which is said to be generally held in the United States, that Texas was included in the cession of Louisiana made by France to the United States in 1803, the undersigned [Rejón] will ask: Can that suffice to invalidate subsequent treaties concluded with due solemnities? By the one which was concluded and signed at Washington on February 22, 1819, between the plenipotentiaries of the United States and Spain, the former recognized the province in question as an integral part of the Spanish provinces; and, if it is now said that such renunciation was improperly made and if it is attempted thereby to base on such belief a right which outweighs that granted by the said treaty; [sic] what guaranty can public conventions afford in the future, when it is easy to allege against all of them some prior right improperly renounced or granted?[19]

This author is in complete agreement with Mexican Foreign Minister Rejón on the sanctity of treaties. As Rejón stated, it is easy to allege against all treaties some right improperly renounced or granted. It is for this reason that this author has never raised, and does not now raise, the question of Texas forming a part of the Louisiana Purchase. Even granting that Texas did form a part of that transaction, the Transcontinental Treaty signed by Secretary of State John Quincy Adams on behalf of the United States and by the Spanish Minister to Washington, Luis de Onís, on behalf of Spain, on February 22,

[19]*Ibid.*, p. 658.

1819 is sufficient to end any and all American pretensions to Texas. Whether John Quincy Adams was correct in agreeing to the Sabine River—as opposed to the Trinity, the Brazos, the Colorado, the Nueces, or the Rio Grande—as the proper boundary between the United States of America and the Viceroyalty of New Spain is not an issue. The fact is that he did agree to such a boundary in exchange for other territorial considerations. The United States gained Florida and an outlet to the Pacific Northwest. Spain gained the Sabine River as a boundary. Having obtained the advantages that were its objectives, the United States could hardly renege on granting Spain the advantages for which it had bargained!

In a similar vein we must consider the Treaty of Velasco, signed by President Santa Anna on behalf of Mexico and by President *ad interim* David G. Burnet on behalf of Texas on May 14, 1836. As a result of that treaty, Santa Anna gained his freedom and the freedom of his troops. Also, a second Mexican army in Texas, commanded by General Vicente Filisola, was allowed to retreat across the Rio Grande unmolested. Texas, for its part, gained recognition as an independent republic from the President of Mexico. That Mexicans in general, and Santa Anna in particular, chose to ignore the Treaty of Velasco after they had obtained their own advantages from it does not invalidate the treaty.

The legality of the Treaty of Velasco has been adequately presented in Chapter 5, and does not need repeating. This author, by mentioning once again the Treaty of Velasco, is simply showing the inconsistent Mexican attitude in regard to legality. When it suited the Mexican fancy to be legalistic, as in the case of the Transcontinental Treaty, the Mexicans became international lawyers. When, however, it did not suit their interests to respect legality, they ran roughshod over treaties or international boundaries with the impunity of bandits!

After belaboring the Transcontinental Treaty of 1819, Rejón went on to another Mexican favorite thesis, the Mexican-American treaty of January 12, 1828. By this treaty the United States recognized the old Spanish-American boundary of the Sabine as the new Mexican-American boundary. From

116

such recognition Foreign Minister Rejón deduced that the United States must be forever frozen in recognizing Mexican sovereignty up to the Sabine. Such "reasoning," of course, would preclude American recognition of the independence of Texas!

While thus challenging the right of the United States to exercise its sovereign power to recognize Texas because the former had once upon a time recognized Mexican sovereignty up to the Sabine, Rejón either never realized or admitted that this same "logic" would have precluded American recognition of Mexican sovereignty up to the Sabine—because the United States had once recognized Spanish sovereignty up to that same river! Apparently it was correct for the United States to substitute Mexican for Spanish sovereignty, but incorrect to substitute Texan for Mexican sovereignty!

If the United States was to be faulted at all, it was for so hastily recognizing the Mexicans. After all, at the time of the Mexican-American treaty of January 12, 1828, Mexico was simply a segment of the Viceroyalty of New Spain in open revolt against its legitimate sovereign, King Fernando VII of Spain. On such grounds it might be argued, using Mexican logic, that the United States had no right to recognize Mexico. As has already been pointed out on two separate occasions, Spain did not deign to recognize the Mexican rebels until December 28, 1836.[20] By the latter date, of course, Mexico was no longer in even *de facto* control of the territory between the Sabine and the Rio Grande. As Spanish recognition of Mexican independence, the *sine qua non* of legitimacy, was obtained only after Mexico ceased to exert even *de facto* control over Texas, Mexico never really held Texas on a *de jure* basis!

Between February 24, 1821, when several provinces of the Viceroyalty of New Spain, Texas included, revolted under the leadership of General Agustín de Iturbide against their Spanish sovereign, and October 3, 1835, when General Antonio López de Santa Anna overthrew what passed for a "government" in Mexico City and destroyed the "Mexican" federal constitution of 1824 that had linked the rebellious Spanish provinces in a confederation, Texas and Mexico had merely been confederates in

[20]Toro, *Compendio de Historia de México*, p. 336.

117

rebellion against Spain. By his destruction of the Mexican confederation on October 3, 1835, Santa Anna severed whatever tenuous links the rebellious Spanish provinces had with each other. Santa Anna, after overthrowing the Mexican confederation, did manage to conquer and hold for his successors most of the territory formerly included in the old confederation of 1824. This territory, however, most assuredly did not include Texas, as the battle of San Jacinto proves. The Treaty of Velasco, then, can be interpreted as an official recognition by Santa Anna that his *de facto* power over certain of the provinces of the Viceroyalty of New Spain did not include Texas.

Whatever the legal status of Texas may have been vis-á-vis Spain, it certainly was of no legitimate concern to Mexico. When the United States finally did annex Texas and the Spanish Government continued to maintain diplomatic relations with the United States, Spanish recognition of the loss of Texas—to the United States—was thus achieved by inaction.

From the foregoing presentation it can be seen that whether a strictly legalistic view regarding the status of Texas is adopted or whether a more *de facto* approach is entertained, Texas was in no way part of Mexico on the eve of the American presidential election of 1844. When the Democratic candidate for President of the United States, James K. Polk, called for the incorporation of Texas into the American Union, he was in no way coveting Mexican territory.

9

The Eve of Polk's Inauguration

James Knox Polk, running on a platform that called for the "reannexation of Texas," was elected President of the United States in November 1844. Meanwhile, in Mexico City the diplomatic correspondence continued. Mexican Foreign Minister Manuel Crescencio Rejón, in the latter part of his October 31, 1844 letter to the American minister, Wilson Shannon, bluntly castigated the government of the United States and Presidents Andrew Jackson and John Tyler in particular. Going beyond the bounds of diplomatic etiquette, Rejón also castigated "the southern people of the United States."

Shannon was not a person to take the Mexican insults as just so much bad manners from a nation that would not admit that a small number of Texans had defeated them. The American minister, in justifiable indignation, informed the offensive Rejón as follows on November 4, 1844:

> The undersigned can hold no communication with the Government of Mexico, unless in terms respectful to himself and to the Government and people, whom he has the honor to represent. The note of H.E. Mr Rejón, repeatedly charges, in terms

the most grossly offensive, the Government and people of the United States with falsehood, artifice, intrigues and designs of a dishonourable character and with bare-faced usurpation. It also charges Genl [Andrew] Jackson, with having, while President of the United States, sent Genl [Sam] Houston to Texas with the secret purpose and dishonourable design of exciting that people to revolt, with the view of procuring the annexation of that territory to the U. States.

These charges are predicated, in part, on a misrepresentation of the note of the undersigned so gross and palpable, and are so often repeated in language so offensive as to manifest a purpose of deliberately insulting the people and Government of the United States. To such changes [sic, charges] so unfounded, made in language so insulting, and for such a purpose, the undersigned can make no reply. He [Shannon] has therefore no alternative but to demand that the note be withdrawn.[1]

The Mexican Foreign Minister answered Shannon two days later with another diatribe. Rejón rejected Shannon's protest and again castigated "The conduct of the Government and the inhabitants of the southern part of the United States." Finally, Rejón refused to withdraw his letter of October 31, 1844, which Shannon had found so offensive, and impudently repeated his support of the offensive document. His last sentence, in fact, was another personal attack on President John Tyler.[2]

On November 8, 1844 Shannon answered Rejón's latest bombast. Shannon informed Rejón that he believed the Mexican's misrepresentations and the reiteration of the unfounded charges and unjust imputations against the American Government and the southern people of the United States were "intended to mislead the public opinion of the people of Mexico, and to excite an unjust prejudice in their minds against the Govt & people of the U. States." Shannon then gave Rejón a lesson in the history of Texas, explaining the events that led up to the independence of the latter republic. He furthermore rejected Rejón's contention "that the Govt and people of the United States have for 20 years entertained a secret purpose and re-

[1] In Manning, *Diplomatic Correspondence of the United States,* VIII, p. 663.
[2] Rejón to Shannon, November 6, 1844, *ibid.,* pp. 664-665.

sorted to improper means for the acquisition of Texas"— which in essence was the basic point of disagreement.[3]

A few days later, on November 12, Shannon apprised Secretary of State Calhoun of his correspondence with Rejón. Shannon let John C. Calhoun know in no uncertain terms that he felt Rejón's letters had been "written for the purpose and with the view, of arousing the jealousies and exciting the prejudices of this [Mexican] people against the Govt & southern people of the U.S., and thereby to make political capital for the party in power [in Mexico City]."[4]

Shannon also reported to Secretary Calhoun that the revolution against General Santa Anna, the current Mexican president, which he had prophesied earlier, had actually commenced. One of the chief instigators of the revolution, which was to prove successful, was General Mariano Paredes y Arrillaga. The new Mexican president, after the overthrow of Santa Anna, would be General José Joaquín de Herrera.

At this point it is necessary to turn to California, in order to bring events in that region into focus. In 1836, partly in support of the Mexican Federal Constitution of 1824 and partly for self-agrandizement, Mariano Guadalupe Vallejo, his nephew Juan Bautista Alvarado, and José Castro staged a revolt against Mexican rule in California. Under the slogan of "Federation or Death," the native Californians removed Governor Nicolás Gutiérrez from office.

By a proclamation issued on November 13, 1836, Juan Bautista Alvarado declared himself governor of California; José Castro prefect of Monterey; and his uncle Mariano Guadalupe Vallejo, whose role in the revolt had not been as active as that of the other two, as military commander. Furthermore, under the native régime:

California was declared to be a free and sovereign state, which would remain separate from Mexico until the Centralist gov-

[3]*Ibid.*, pp. 666-668.
[4]*Ibid.*, p. 677.

ernment was overthrown and the Constitution of 1824 was again adopted by all the Mexican states.[5]

Later, in order to guarantee his power and quiet the budding sectional rivalry between northern and southern California, Governor Alvarado agreed to accept the new *centralista* Constitutional Laws of December 30, 1836.

Unfortunately for the quasi-independent state of California, however, the quarrels of rival families and the jealousies between its northern and southern sections continued. The strength of the new revolutionary régime of Governor Juan Bautista Alvarado was based in the north, around Monterey, San José, and San Francisco Bay. The Mexico City officials exploited a north-south cleavage to maintain some facade of their former authority. In spite of this, however, Mexico's grasp on California by 1840 is best described as weak and precarious. It was not until 1841 that the Mexicans were able to reassert their former authority.

With the overthrow of the government of General Anastasio Bustamante in Mexico City in 1841, General Santa Anna had returned to the presidency of Mexico. Santa Anna soon sent 300 convict-troops, under the command of General Manuel Micheltorena, to subjugate California. For a few years General Micheltorena remained as the Mexican-imposed military governor of California. In the interim his convict-soldiers, who maintained him in power, "robbed hen-roosts or whatever else they could lay hands on."[6] However, American immigrants continued coming into California in steadily increasing numbers.

In the middle of November 1844 the native Californians pronounced against the Micheltorena régime. In order to bolster his military position vis-á-vis the Californians, General Micheltorena enlisted the mercenary aid of Johann August Sutter, a naturalized Mexican who had come from Switzerland, and of Isaac Graham, a native of Tennessee. Because of the aid rendered by Sutter, Graham, and about a hundred Americans

[5]George Lockhart Rives, *The United States and Mexico: 1821-1848*, (2 vols., New York: Scribner's, 1913), II, p. 33; hereafter cited as Rives, *U.S. and Mexico*.

[6]*Ibid.*, p. 39.

and English, plus some Indians, Micheltorena and his force of some 300 Mexicans were able to force the Californian rebels under Juan Bautista Alvarado and José Castro to stage an initial retreat. The Californians, at this juncture, numbered only about 90 men.

In spite of this initial success, however, General Micheltorena lost the final round and on February 21, 1845 capitulated to the Californians. The following day Micheltorena signed a treaty with the Californian rebels whereby he agreed that he and his convict-soldiers would return to Mexico and a native Californian, Pío Pico, would become governor *ad interim* of California. Furthermore, José Castro became military commander of California, and Juan Bautista Alvarado was given the customs house at Monterey.

As events turned out, General Micheltorena's defeat and ouster in California coincided with the overthrow of the Santa Anna régime in Mexico City. The new Mexican government of General José Joaquín de Herrera was not at all displeased with the overthrow of Micheltorena, who was Santa Anna's man. It might be mentioned, however, that while the new Herrera government was approving the ouster of the *santannista* general, it was also taking steps to restore Mexican authority in California. Some 600 men, with large quantities of supplies, were placed under the command of a Colonel Ignacio Iniestra. This force, which was apparently intended to invade California and restore Mexican rule, got only as far as Cuernavaca before the successful Paredes revolution broke out on December 14, 1845.

California, it might be added, had not escaped international notice. Waddy Thompson, then United States minister to Mexico, wrote on April 29, 1842 to then Secretary of State Daniel Webster that ". . . California is destined to be the granary of the Pacific. It is a country in which slavery is not necessary. . . . France and England both have had their eyes upon it;—The latter has yet."[7]

In 1841 the British minister in Mexico, Sir Richard Pakenham, was concerned about the possibilities of French activities in California. Pakenham became especially suspicious about the

[7]In Manning, *Diplomatic Correspondence of the United States*, VIII, p. 484.

journies of one Duplot du Morfras, an attaché of the French legation at Mexico, who during the years 1841, 1842, and 1843 traveled extensively in California. Pakenham was in communication with a James Alexander Forbes, who considered California as a field for foreign, that is, British, colonization. Pakenham further wrote to Lord Palmerston, the British Foreign Minister, on August 30, 1841, advocating British settlement of California.[8]

By September 1844 Forbes, now British consul at Monterey, California, was in communication with the British consul at Tepic, Mexico, a Mr. Barron, on the subject of establishing a British protectorate over California. Barron kept Lord Aberdeen, now British Foreign Minister, informed on this topic. Lord Aberdeen stated that Great Britain would "view with much dissatisfaction the establishment of a protectoral power over California by any other foreign state."[9] The British, however, unwilling to collide miliatrily with the United States and uncertain of the attitude of France, in the last analysis remained passive regarding California.

[8]In Ephraim Douglas Adams, "English Interests in the Annexation of California," *The American Historical Review*, XIV, No. 4 (July, 1909), p. 745.

[9]Lord Aberdeen to Barron, Dec. 31, 1844, *ibid.*, p. 752.

10
Letters from Mexico

With the election of James Knox Polk to the presidency of the United States, events began to move more rapidly. In February 1845 the American Congress approved a joint resolution inviting Texas to join the Union. On March 1, 1845 President Tyler, in one of his final acts as President, signed the joint resolution of Congress. On March 4, 1845 James K. Polk was inaugurated as the eleventh President of the United States.

General Juan N. Almonte, the Mexican minister to the United States, angered over the American invitation to Texas to join the Union, broke off diplomatic relations between Mexico and the United States on March 6, 1845, just two days after President Polk's inauguration.

On March 28, 1845 Luis G. Cuevas, now Foreign Minister of Mexico in the Herrera government, informed the American minister in Mexico, Wilson Shannon, about the break in diplomatic relations between Mexico and the United States. At the same time that Foreign Minister Cuevas was breaking off United States-Mexican diplomatic relations, he circulated a note to the British, French, and Spanish ministers in Mexico City. In this note Cuevas informed the three European ministers that Mexico would go to war against the United States in order to oppose the incorporation of Texas into the American Union.[1]

Wilson Shannon, in one of his last official acts as Minister of the United States to Mexico, informed the new American Secretary of State, James Buchanan, of Cuevas' rupture of diplomatic relations and also sent Buchanan a copy of Cuevas' note to the British, French, and Spanish ministers.[2] The United States government was now officially informed once again of the hostile intent of Mexico.

President Polk, in spite of Mexican hostility, sent a confidential agent, Dr. William S. Parrott, to Mexico to endeavor to learn if a peaceful solution to the American-Mexican disagreement over Texas could be achieved. On April 26, 1845 Dr. Parrott wrote Secretary of State James Buchanan from Mexico:

> One thing however is quite manifest in all quarters, that of an intense excitement among all parties and classes on the question of the annexation of Texas to the United States; such, in fact, is the intensity of this excitement that it would be difficult for any party to remain long in power, who did not participate in it; professedly at least—
>
> War with the United States seems to be the desire of all parties, rather than see Texas annexed to the U.S.[3]

Shortly thereafter Dr. Parrott again wrote the Secretary of State:

> The excitement against the Government and people of the United States, of which you were advised in my former letters, still prevails, although I am inclined to believe, not with the same intensity—The opposition presses serve to keep alive the war spirit of the people. The present administration [of General José Joaquín de Herrera] is both timid and vacilating—Changes in the cabinet, must inevitably follow, if in the foreign Department so much the better, as it is now sold to the British interest, and cannot be approached by us. . . .

[1] In Manning, *Diplomatic Correspondence of the United States,* VIII, p. 707; Bosch Garcia, *La Historia Diplomática de México,* p. 487.

[2] Shannon to Buchanan, April 6, 1845, in Manning, *Diplomatic Correspondence of the United States,* VIII, p. 709.

[3] *Ibid.,* p. 712.

The opposition to the present administration professes to be very anxious for a war with the U.S. as you will perceive from the files of papers, which I forward by the present conveyance; but it is not sincere. It wants place and power, and I am inclined to believe it will have them. . . .

Great Britain has greatly increased her Naval Forces in the Pacific, the object of which, *as stated,* is, to take possession of, and hold upper California, in case of a war between the U.S. & Mexico—to secure the interests of some of her subjects in a mortgage on a nominal part of that Territory."[4]

On May 22, 1845 Dr. Parrott informed Buchanan about a report which a committee of the Mexican Senate had issued. The report, dated May 14, 1845, read:

1st. The Mexican nation convokes all her sons to the defence of the national independence, menaced by the usurpation of the Texan territory attempted by the decree of annexation given by Congress and sanctioned by the President of the United States of the North. 2nd. Consequently the government shall put under arms all the force of the permanent and active militia, in conformity to the authorization conceded to it, by the existing laws; for the preservation of Public order, support of the institutions, and in case of necessity, it shall employ the army as a reserve: & exercising the power conceded to it . . . it shall raise the forces mentioned therein, under the name of defenders of the independence and laws.[5]

While President Polk's confidential agent in Mexico City was thus keeping the administration informed of events, Thomas O. Larkin, the United States consul at Monterey, California, wrote an interesting letter describing events in California. Because of the distance involved, Larkin was apparently unaware of the name of the new American Secretary of State, as he addressed his letter to the former Secretary, John C. Calhoun. Larkin stated:

The situation of California and its Government under the

[4]May 13, 1845, *ibid.*, pp. 715-716.
[5]May 22, 1845, *ibid.*, p. 717.

natives of the country continues in a quiet state; having risen against the Mexican General [Manuel Micheltorena] and shipped him and all his forces to San Blas, the people have distributed the different offices among themselves, with the firm determination of resisting every attempt of Mexico to change the face of affairs in this Department, while the President of Mexico will allow the Californians to govern their own country, they will use the Mexican Flag, obey such of her Laws as may be applicable to the country, enter goods in the Custom House, when they find the article not prohibited and put their own duties on when it is; her Laws will be abrogated or complyed [sic] with, as it may meet their views.

Larkin further reported that the British vice consul at Monterey, acting as agent for the British Hudson Bay Co., had apparently recognized the "new government" of the California rebels. According to Larkin, the British vice consul had presented a bill to the California rebels, due the Hudson Bay Co., "for powder, ball, lances &c. supplied at the outset of the revolution, by the late Agent, which bill has been accepted and payment promised. . . ." Larkin then stated that the British vice consul had hoisted his flag and fired a salute upon publication of the announcement that the Mexican general, Manuel Micheltorena, had been overthrown, and that the rebels were in charge. Larkin also implied that this British vice consul, whom he neglected to name, was involved in the revolution, having sided with the California rebels.[6]

On June 10, 1845, Dr. Parrott was again writing James Buchanan. The American Secretary of State was informed that the Mexican national congress had passed a resolution declaring that the "unjust despoliation" of Texas by the United States gave Mexico "the right to employ all its means and power to resist, to the utmost peril, the said annexation. . . ."[7]

On the same day, John Black, the American consul at Mexico City, wrote Secretary of State Buchanan that the Mexican congress had decreed the following:

[6]Larkin to Calhoun, June 6, 1845, *ibid.*, pp. 721-722.
[7]*Ibid.*, p. 725.

1. The Mexican Nation convokes all its sons to the defence of the national independence, threatened by the usurpation, of the territory of Texas, which is attempted to be realized by the decree of annexation, given by the Chambers, and sanctioned by the President of the United States of the North,

2. In consequence the Government shall put under arms all the forces of the Army according to the Authority conceded to it by existing laws, for the preservation of public order, to sustain the institutions, and in case it should be necessary to serve as a reserve to the Army, the Government in use of the power conceded to it, on the 9th of December 1844—may raise the troops of which the same decree speaks under the name of Defenders of the Independence, and of the laws.[8]

A less warlike attitude on the part of Mexico was soon reported to Buchanan, however. Parrott wrote the Secretary of State that:

. . . I have been able to ascertain that an act declaratory of war with the United States cannot pass [the Mexican] Congress, should it be even urged by the Executive. . . . It is therefore very certain that a declaration of war by Mexico, is not at all probable, I might add, not seriously thought of. There is not a reasonable man in power or in representation among them, who does not give up Texas as lost to them, by its annexation to the United States; and many of those with whom I have conversed, (they now converse with greater freedom on this sore subject, than when I first arrived among them) say, that whenever the excitement caused by annexation shall have subsided, an endeavor, on the part of this Government, will be made to obtain the best possible arrangement with that of the U.S. in compensation for their loss. This endeavor, I have assured them on all suitable occasions, would, in my opinion, be met by the Government at Washington, in a friendly and liberal spirit—[9]

On June 29, 1845 Dr. Parrott, writing to Secretary of State James Buchanan, expressed the hope "that the main object of my mission will be accomplished, namely that of preventing a declaration of war, by Mexico, against the United States."[10] This

[8]*Ibid.*, p. 726.
[9]June 24, 1845, *ibid.*, p. 730.

129

author believes that this particular sentence, written by President Polk's confidential agent in Mexico to Polk's secretary of state, gives a clear indication that the Polk Administration was desirous of peace with Mexico. So eager, in fact, was President Polk to avoid war with Mexico that he had speedily dispatched Dr. Parrott to Mexico City in quest of peace. It might be pointed out that the ship that took Parrott to Mexico also carried General Juan N. Almonte, only recently Mexican minister to the United States, so great was the speed with which the new Polk Administration moved to resume relations with Mexico.

On the theme of the Polk Administration's peaceful intentions regarding Mexico, it is interesting to read Bosch García's synopsis of Secretary of State James Buchanan's letter of March 28, 1845, to Dr. Parrott:

> James Buchanan attempted to reestablish the broken relations with Mexico by means of his confidential agent, William S. Parrott, to whom he explained the following: The United States wished to reestablish relations, if possible, within a frame of national honor for them [the United States]. Parrott was the one selected to reestablish them, and the success of his mission depended on the consideration and prudence which he had. He would probably have obtained better results if he had not made known to the Mexican government that he was an official agent of North America, unless it became absolutely necessary. He hoped that his long residence in Mexico and his knowledge of the Mexican mentality favored his effort. His mission consisted of entering into contact with the members of the government and convincing them that it was to Mexico's interest to reestablish relations with the United States, and once convinced, have them know that the United States was prepared to send a representative who would be named as soon as it was found out that he would be received in a dignified manner.[11]

Writing to Secretary of State Buchanan on July 5, 1845, Dr. Parrott stated:

> Within the last few days the press generally has been more vituperative of us, than it had been for some weeks before,

[10]*Ibid.*
[11]In Bosch García, *La Historia Diplomática de México*, p. 487.

which is owing to the endeavor of British influence to make believe that, a war between the United States and England, growing out of the Oregon question, is inevitable—Such a hope, if entertained by Mexico, may very materially change her contemplated policy toward the United States, and retard the renewal of her friendly and Diplomatic relations with us.[12]

Meanwhile, from Thomas O. Larkin, in Monterey, California, came more information concerning that region. It will be recalled that in Chapter 9, the intentions of the Mexican government to oust the rebel California authorities by sending Colonel Ignacio Iniestra with 600 troops were first mentioned. On this subject Larkin told Buchanan "that the newly established Government of Mexico are fitting out at Acapulco, an expedition of troops for the purpose of putting out of office, the California Officers and reinstating the Authorities of Mexico."

Larkin continued:

> The present native Government of California were provided in part with arms and money, by Mr. William Rea, the Agent of the Hudson Bay Company in this Country last October and November when the Californians rose against General [Manuel] Micheltorena: Mr. Rea and his Clerk, both Englishmen, were on the field when the Californians and Mexicans made a treaty binding General Micheltorena, to send out of California all his troops within ninety days. . . . Mr. Rea's Clerk received a commission of Ensign under the Californians, since this period the Agent has shot himself.

The game the British government was playing in California is rather muddled, however because Larkin, in the same letter, states:

> There is no doubt in this Country, but the Troops now expected here in September are sent on by the instigation of the English Government under the plea, that the American settlers in California want to revolutionize the Country, [sic] it is rumoured, that two English [Banking] houses in Mexico, have

[12] In Manning, *Diplomatic Correspondence of the United States*, VIII, pp. 733-734.

become bound to the new [Mexican] General to accept his drafts for funds to pay his Troops for eighteen months.[13]

On July 12, 1845 Dr. Parrott informed Secretary of State Buchanan that the Mexican government seemed, at times, to entertain sole thought of declaring war against the United States in the event that Texas should join the American Union. Parrott went on to say that he had been waited upon by a relative of one of the Mexican Secretaries, who wished to find out what the United States would do in the event that Mexico should declare war, without actually accompanying the declaration with any act of hostility. Parrott stated that he answered the Mexican that, *in his opinion,* the United States would act "with promptness and energy; knowing the true interests of both countries required a speedy restoration of that mutual confidence and good neighbourhood which should subsist between neighboring states." Dr. Parrott then concluded his letter by telling Buchanan that the opposition to the Mexican government:

> . . . continues to be prodigal of assurances, that the necessary means will not be wanting to prosecute the [proposed] war to a successful termination, and thus to save the national honor. But with all this I cannot believe the extremity of war will be resorted to. The presumption and folly of this people are great, it is true; but hardly enough so, to force the administration to adopt a measure, which if persisted in, might, ere long endanger the national existence of their country.[14]

It might be pointed out that "the opposition" at this time was led by General Mariano Paredes y Arrillaga, who ultimately overthrew the Herrera government and replaced General Herrera in the presidency in January 1846.

On July 19, 1845 John Black, the United States consul at Mexico City wrote Secretary of State James Buchanan that from the proceedings of the Mexican government "it would appear, and is generally believed here, that a declaration of war against the United States is inevitable." Black concluded by speculating as follows:

[13]July 10, 1845, *ibid.*, pp. 735-736.
[14]*Ibid.*, p. 737.

132

I think it is now the intention of this Government to carry on the war against Texas without making a formal declaration against the United States, in this way she thinks she will save her honor and not expose herself to an immediate attack on her sea board.[15]

A few days later Dr. William S. Parrott wrote to Buchanan that the members of the Mexican Cabinet had presented a statement to their congress which declared:

From the moment the [Mexican] Government knows that the Department of Texas has annexed itself to the American union, or that the Department had been invaded by the troops of the [American] union, the [Mexican] nation shall be declared at war with the United States of North America.[16]

Keeping Buchanan abreast of the situation, Dr. Parrott wrote on July 30, that Mexico:

. . . will concentrate all the force she can, on the Frontier of Texas (*she is now doing so, and the command is given to Genl. Filisola*) in the hope of making a run, upon the defenceless inhabitants; thus entertain the question until England can be heard from, which she *believes* will lend a helping hand, and if not, she will then be willing to negotiate, or *arbitrate,* at the instance of some *friendly power.*[17]

This letter was soon followed by another, on August 5, in which Dr. Parrott reiterated his belief that "a *run* will be made upon Texas." In this same letter Dr. Parrott stated that "Another portion of the force destined to California has left for Acapulco, to embark; Col. Yuristra [*sic,* Col. Ignacio Iniestra], it is said will soon follow."[18]

On August 16, 1845 Dr. Parrott wrote Buchanan that Mexico had a new minister of foreign relations, Manuel de la Peña y Peña. More important, Dr. Parrott claimed that General José

[15]*Ibid.* p. 739.
[16]Parrott to Buchanan, July 22, 1845, *ibid.,* p. 740.
[17]*Ibid.,* p. 744.
[18]*Ibid.,* p. 745.

Joaquín de Herrera, the Mexican president, appeared to be in favor of friendly relations with the United States. Dr. Parrott further stated that General Herrera would be prepared to receive American commissioners.

Dr. Parrott wrote again on August 26, stating that the Mexican government desired to settle the differences with the United States by negotiation. Unfortunately, it could not act freely because of an obstinate opposition to all its measures. Dr. Parrott further mentioned that General Mariano Paredes y Arrillaga, who had been summoned to Mexico City, had satisfied the Mexican government by sending commissioners.

Regarding California, Secretary of State Buchanan was informed that the Californians had sent commissioners to Mexico City who had told the central government that "they will not receive supplies of *men* from the central power; that they can defend themselves, and that all they want, are, arms and ammunition—This looks as if they were disposed to set up *business* on their *own* account."[19]

Dr. Parrott then returned to the theme of Texas and informed James Buchanan that a Mexican declaration of war against the United States was no longer spoken of. Furthermore, Parrott stated that a desire existed, even publicly manifested, to receive a commissioner from the United States. Parrott concluded his letter by stating that the insubordination of General Vicente Filisola's command, which instead of marching to the Texas frontier had marched back, had found its way to the command of General Paredes. Parrott mentioned that it was feared that the insubordinate officers would march on Mexico City.

John Black, writing to Secretary of State Buchanan on September 2, 1845, reported that California had asked the Mexican government to re-establish the federal constitution of 1824. Black also stated that the expedition under Colonel Ignacio Iniestra, by which the Mexican central government hoped to subdue the Californians, still remained in the capital. Black then told Buchanan about the incipient plot to overthrow the Mexican government:

[19]*Ibid.*, p. 747.

. . . a plan has been forming by the Military at the head of which are Generals Paredes and Tornel, the object of which is to overthrow the present government, and to establish in its stead a Military Triumvirate, and although the Government has endeavored, to impress the public with the idea, that, it has every confidence in the fidelity of General Paredes, yet it is believed that it has undoubted information in its possession, that he has been planning for its overthrow. . . . [20]

Dr. Parrott, in a letter dated September 13, ominously informed Buchanan that the official newspaper of the Herrera government "which has been silent for several weeks on the subject of war with the United States, came out yesterday, more hostile than is its wont to be." Parrott surmised that the reason for the more hostile tone was to pacify General Mariano Paredes y Arrillaga and to weaken his command.[21]

Concerning the confused state of affairs in California, Larkin soon informed Secretary Buchanan as follows:

The Government of California is now held by two parties, one in Monterey under Castro and Alvarado, the other under Governor Pio Pico in the Town of the Angels [Los Angeles], four hundred miles South of this Port, these two parties small as they are, cannot agree, and affairs are becoming worse between them in such a manner, that the people hardly care what Flag is exchanged for their own.[22]

In what seemed to be a breakthrough in diplomatic negotiations, Manuel de la Peña y Peña informed John Black that the Mexican government was "disposed to receive the commissioner of the United States, who may come to this Capital, with full powers from his Government, to settle the present dispute, in a peaceful reasonable and honourable manner."[23]

John Black was soon writing to Secretary James Buchanan that "The Mexican Government is very anxious to know when

[20]*Ibid.*, p. 749.
[21]*Ibid.*, pp. 751-752.
[22]Sept. 29, 1845, *ibid.*, p. 755.
[23]Oct. 15, 1845, *ibid.*, p. 763.

they may expect the Envoy from the United States, and also that I may soon be able to give it the information, of the American Squadron having retired from the Port of Vera Cruz."[24]

As a result of the highly provocative diplomatic attitude of the Mexican government that appeared in the Mexican newspapers and Mexico's action in ordering troops to the Texas frontier, the administration of President Polk had seen fit to send a naval squadron into the Gulf of Mexico off Veracruz. This squadron, under the command of Commodore David Conner, which was prepared to defend Texas against a Mexican assault, aroused the obvious displeasure of the Mexican officials. This was the squadron that Mexican Foreign Minister Peña y Peña had requested be removed.

With the apparent thawing in Mexican-American relations and a seeming desire on the part of Mexico to receive an American envoy to negotiate peace, Commodore Conner withdrew from Veracruz. On October 29, 1845 Black was able to inform Peña y Peña of Conner's withdrawal and to enclose a copy of the commodore's letter to F. M. Dimond, the United States consul at Veracruz.

Conner's letter, dated October 23 and written aboard the U.S. Ship *Falmouth,* read:

> Sir: By the letter of Mr. Black, which you were kind enough to send me this morning, I learn that the proposition, to enter into Negotiation, made by our Government to that of this Country, had been accepted. There appears to exist, on the part of this Government, some fear least they should be accused of being forced into this measure, by the hostile attitude of the U. States.
>
> Being fully aware that our Government, has had no intention of threatening this Country, but, on the contrary, has always been actuated by a sincere desire to treat existing differences, in a manner honorable to both nations, I believe that I shall best contribute to such an arrangement by withdrawing our Naval force from before Vera Cruz—
>
> I am Very Respectfully (etc.).[25]

[24]Oct. 28, 1845, *ibid.,* p. 768.
[25]*Ibid.,* p. 769.

11
Polk Strives for Peace

As a direct result of the Black-Peña y Peña communications, President Polk sent John Slidell to Mexico City to negotiate with the Herrera government. Slidell went ashore at Veracruz on November 29, 1845, and the news of his arrival was known to Black on December 3. The unusual speed with which Slidell had been appointed and sent to Mexico following Foreign Minister Manuel de la Peña y Peña's October 15 affirmation that Mexico would receive a United States commissioner was not to the liking of the Herrera government. When John Black called on Peña y Peña to inform him of Slidell's arrival at Veracruz, the foreign minister was very upset and bluntly told Black: "You know the opposition are calling us traitors for entering into this arrangement with you."[1]

On Saturday, December 6, 1845 John Slidell reached Mexico City, and on Monday, December 8, he wrote to Foreign Minister Peña y Peña requesting that he be received by the President of Mexico, General José Joaquín de Herrera. Not receiving an answer, Slidell wrote again on December 15. On December 20, Foreign Minister Peña y Peña officially informed Slidell that he

[1] Black to Buchanan, Dec. 18, 1845, in U.S., Cong., *Exec. Doc.* 60, H.R., 30th Cong., 1st sess., p. 23.

would not be received, after the Mexican newspapers had two days earlier published the refusal of the Herrera government to receive him.[2]

In refusing to present him to General Herrera, Peña y Peña based his reasoning on the sole ground that Slidell had been commissioned as an envoy extraordinary and minister plenipotentiary, rather than as a commissioner, and suggested that Slidell obtain new credentials.[3]

While Slidell was in Mexico City the long-expected revolt of General Mariano Paredes y Arrillaga broke out. As Manuel de la Peña y Peña had predicted, the mere fact that the government of General Herrera had permitted a plenipotentiary of the United States to enter Mexico was put at the head of the list of grievances by the Paredes forces.

General Mariano Paredes y Arrillaga raised the standard of revolt on December 14, 1845 at San Luis Potosí, and on December 31 General José Joaquín de Herrera resigned the presidency of Mexico. On January 3, 1846 General Paredes became the new President of Mexico. The next day General Paredes publicly swore to "defend the integrity of the national territory, and this had reference to Texas—every foot of Texas to the Sabine—for such was the unqualified claim of Mexico."[4]

John Slidell continued to stay in Mexico, hoping that perhaps the new government of General Paredes would receive him. On March 1, Slidell wrote to Joaquín de Castillo y Lanzas, the foreign minister in the Paredes government. Castillo y Lanzas answered Slidell on March 12, refusing to see him, and declared that this decision was "immutable." In this same letter the foreign minister admitted that the Mexican government was "preparing for war, should circumstances require it," but also stated that it would keep alive its "flattering hope" for peace.[5] As there was no longer any point in remaining in Mexico, John Slidell requested his passports from Castillo y Lanzas and upon their receipt on March 21, 1846 prepared to leave.

[2]*Ibid.*, p. 38.

[3]*Ibid.*, pp. 38-39.

[4]Smith, *The War with Mexico*, I, p. 100.

[5]In Manning, *Diplomatic Correspondence of the United States*, VIII, pp. 821-823.

George Lockhart Rives, in *The United States and Mexico: 1821-1848,* states:

> The action of the two successive Mexican administrations in refusing to receive an American minister ended all further discussion. Their decision had plainly been dictated by the exigencies of domestic politics. The opinions of the governing class had been too clearly declared to make it possible for any government to enter at that time upon negotiations with the United States; and although the men who were actually intrusted with the responsibility of carrying on the affairs of the republic must have had some perception of the inevitable result of a conflict, they could not have remained in office for a single day if they had openly defied the public clamor for war.[6]

Concerning President Polk's peaceful intentions, Robert Toombs, then a Whig member of Congress and later the first Secretary of State of the Southern Confederacy, stated in February 1846: "Mr. Polk never dreamed of any other war than a war upon the Whigs."[7]

Daniel Webster—a former Secretary of State, one of the leaders of the Whig opposition to President Polk, and an advocate of peace during the Mexican War—stated prior to hostilities: "That Mr. Polk and his Cabinet will desire to keep the peace, there is no doubt. The responsibility of having provoked war by their scheme of annexation is what they would greatly dread."[8]

Furthermore, General Winfield Scott, the commander of the army, was a Whig and a recognized candidate for the presidency. Both President Polk and the other chieftains of the Democratic party fully comprehended that a war might result in General Scott's succeeding Polk at the next election. War expenses, in addition, would result in higher taxes and the strengthening of the tariff system, which a great number of Democrats found obnoxious.

[6]Rives, *U.S. and Mexico*, II, p. 80.
[7]Smith, *The War with Mexico*, I, P. 130.
[8]*Ibid.*

As things turned out, President Polk was succeeded by Zachary Taylor, a Whig general made famous by the very war Polk hoped to avoid.

In fact, one of the very first acts of the Polk administration had been to send Dr. William S. Parrott to Mexico as a confidential agent in order to work for the re-establishment of the diplomatic relations between Mexico and the United States that the Mexicans had broken over President John Tyler's annexation of Texas. As already mentioned, the same ship that took Dr. Parrott to Mexico also carried General Juan N. Almonte, the late Mexican minister to the United States, so great was the speed with which President Polk had moved to resume relations with Mexico.

While President Polk was desirous of peace, he nonetheless took precautionary steps to protect the United States in the event the Mexicans should provoke a war. In particular, various naval units were sent to patrol the waters off Mexico.

General Zachary Taylor's advance to the Rio Grande was a highly expedient move. First of all, the American claim to the region between the Nueces and the Rio Grande would have been weakened had the United States not been physically present. Second, as has been proven earlier, the territory between the two rivers belonged to Texas and hence to the United States after annexation.[9] Third, the Rio Grande region represented a better strategic position than did the Nueces, should Mexico's threat of war be carried into effect. Finally, it was believed that a bold and militant attitude on the part of the United States would sober the Mexicans and serve to facilitate negotiation.

John Slidell, who was in Mexico City when the Paredes revolt broke out, felt that the advance of General Taylor to the Rio Grande and the strengthening of our naval squadron in the Gulf might exercise a mollifying effect on the course of the Paredes government.[10]

[9]See chapter 6, "The Texas Boundary."
[10]Slidell to Buchanan, Feb. 17, 1846, in Manning, *Diplomatic Correspondence of the United States*, VIII, p. 813.

Justin Harvey Smith points out that:

> When the Mexican government gave formal notice to England and France in the summer of 1845 that war [with the United States] had become inevitable, our army lay far from the Rio Grande. Taylor's advance to the Bold River no more produced the war than Pitcairn's march to Lexington produced the American revolution. It was an effect and an occasion, but not a cause.
>
> Finally, as a matter of fact, the hostilities were deliberately precipitated by the will and act of Mexico.[11]

In support of this thesis, Smith quotes, among others, Mariano Otero, editor of the Mexican newspaper *El Siglo XIX* and senator from the state of Jalisco, and the Mexican general Mariano Arista. In October 1847 Senator Otero stated:

> The American forces did not advance to the Rio Grande until after the war became inevitable, and then only as an army of observation. . . . The military rebellion of San Luis [Potosí] gave rise to a government [that of Paredes] pledged to resist all accommodation [with the United States] . . . which government [Paredes'] began hostilities.[12]

General Arista declared in December 1847: "I had the pleasure of being the first to begin the war."[13]

Before concluding this chapter it might be appropriate to mention John Charles Frémont's expedition to California in 1845-1846, conducted under the aegis of the Topographical Bureau. It has been alleged by some historians, either misinformed or seeking to discredit President Polk, that Frémont explorations in search of the shortest route to Oregon did in truth constitute an "invasion" of Mexico. Any examination of the origins of the Mexican War, then, must of necessity briefly report on this little group of 60 civilians who, along with

[11]Smith, *The War with Mexico*, I, pp. 154-155.
[12]*Ibid.*, p. 155.
[13]*Ibid.*

Frémont—an engineer—were employed by the Topographical Bureau.

On the eve of the Mexican War, California was governed by a group of native Californians whose claim to power was based on revolution. These self-constituted authorities, whose chief leaders were Juan Bautista Alvarado, José Castro, and Pío Pico, had set up what amounted to an independent state, giving only lip service to Mexican sovereignty. At best they were an irregular *junta*, barely tolerated by Mexico. It has also been shown that the government of General Herrera in Mexico City had attempted to remove the California rebels from power by sending regular Mexican troops under Colonel Ignacio Iniestra. The ensuing Paredes revolution against Herrera, however, and the war against the United States served to abort Colonel Iniestra's invasion, thus allowing the California rebels to retain their offices.

When Frémont and his small party entered California, intent on scientific undertakings, they somehow ran afoul of General José Castro, one of the rebel triumvirate then constituting the government of California.

Regarding Frémont, it is appropriate to mention that, subsequent to his scientific explorations in California, he attained the rank of major during the Mexican War, but came into conflict with General Stephen Watts Kearny, the American general who had been given command of the Army of the West. For this conflict with General Kearny, Frémont was arrested for mutiny and insubordination and subsequently courtmartialed. Years later, as a major general in the Union army during the Civil War, Frémont emancipated the slaves in the area under the control of his troops. For this he was reprimanded by President Abraham Lincoln, and his act was rescinded by the President.

Regarding General José Castro, the rebel military commandant of California at the time of Frémont's arrival, it should be noted that he had already distinguished himself as a chief instigator in the rebellion against the last Mexican governor of California, General Manuel Micheltorena. General Castro, furthermore, was in conflict with his fellow revolutionary, Pío Pico, the rebel governor of California.

The point being made here is that the Frémont-Castro conflict is best seen as a dispute between two rather difficult personalities, neither of whom had the blessing of his own government.

For those interested in Frémont's explorations and adventures, this author might suggest Frémont's own *Colonel John Charles Frémont, and His Narrative of Explorations and Adventures, in Kansas, Nebraska, Oregon and California* (New York: Miller, Orten & Mulligan, 1856); John Bigelow's *Memoir of The Life And Public Service of John Charles Frémont* (New York: Derby & Jackson, 1856); or Allan Nevins' *Frémont: Pathmarker of the West* (New York: Appleton-Century, 1939).

Returning to James K. Polk and his attempt to find a peaceful solution to the disagreement with Mexico, it can be clearly seen that the President was not responsible for the activities of the adventurous Mr. Frémont.

Finally, John Slidell, before leaving Mexico, made known to the Paredes government that the United States was willing to relieve the Mexicans from pecuniary embarrassment if they would do us justice regarding the boundary.[14] These are hardly the words of a diplomat whose government was intent on war.

---

[14]Slidell to Buchanan, Apr. 2, 1846, in Manning, *Diplomatic Correspondence of the United States*, VIII, p. 837.

12
Paredes and War

General Mariano Paredes y Arrillaga, who assumed the presidency of Mexico on January 3, 1846, had long been in communication with his fellow generals regarding a war with the United States.[1] On April 14, 1846, General Pedro de Ampudia wrote General Paredes concerning a plan of attack. According to General Ampudia, the Americans under General Zachary Taylor could be defeated "within the space of four days," as General Anastasio Torrejón was arriving that night with the division of operations.[2] General Ampudia complained, however, that General Mariano Arista had been named to replace him as general-in-chief of the Mexican forces in the north. General Ampudia was quite bitter, indeed, that General Arista would direct the campaign.[3]

General Ampudia had, previous to his letter to General Paredes, begun preparations for war by ordering, on April 11,

[1]Mariano Paredes y Arrillaga Papers, 1844-1846, García Collection, University of Texas Archives, Latin American Collection, Austin, Texas; hereafter cited as Paredes Papers.

[2]Ampudia to Paredes, Apr. 14, 1846, in Paredes Papers, Wallet 145, number 114.

[3]*Ibid.*

1846, the United States consul at Matamoros, Peter Schatzell, and all American citizens residing there to leave Matamoros "within the precise term of twenty four hours, destined for the City of Victoria." General Ampudia had further stated "that a like order would be given in respect to the Americans residing in the other towns on the frontier, and that all Americans who may be found to have passed to the left bank of the River [Rio Grande], shall be shot within an hour after [being] taken."[4]

John Black, the United States consul in Mexico City, in a letter to Foreign Minister Joaquín de Castillo y Lanzas protested General Ampudia's order, which nevertheless was executed. Black pointed out that this was "a most flagrant violation" of treaty stipulations, citing the 26th article of the Treaty of Amity, Commerce, and Navigation that the United States of America and the United Mexican States had concluded on April 5, 1835. Black apprised Foreign Minister Castillo y Lanzas that, even in the extremity of war, the treaty stipulated that merchants on the coast were to be given six months, and those in the interior one year, " 'to arrange their business [and] dispose of their effects, or transport them wheresoever they may please, giving them safe conduct, to protect them to the port they may designate.' "[5]

Castillo y Lanzas, who showed the same disregard for legality that his compatriots had evinced throughout the period covered by this work, dismissed Black's protest on the flimsy pretense that Black, a mere consul, did not have diplomatic standing, and it was thus not his function to make protests of such a character.[6]

On April 24, 1846 General Mariano Arista, who had just replaced General Pedro de Ampudia as general-in-chief of the Mexican forces in the north, wrote to General Paredes concerning his own attack plans. General Paredes was informed that General Anastasio Torrejón would cross over to the left bank of the Rio Bravo [Rio Grande] with 1200 cavalry and 400 infantry. General Arista continued:

[4]Black to Castillo y Lanzas, May 1, 1846, in Manning, *Diplomatic Correspondence of the United States*, VIII, p. 846.
[5]*Ibid.*
[6]May 5, 1846, *ibid.*, p. 849.

Consequently, we already have sixteen hundred men, who this very day perhaps will begin to fight the enemy by every possible means, cutting his communications between the frontier and Corpus Cristi, destroying his cavalry and narrowing him more and more into the pocket where he has been placed.

I arrive today at Matamoros, where I now have ready two thousand infantrymen with whom I shall cross to the other side of the Bravo [Rio Grande] protected by Mr. [General] Torrejón, with the object of giving a decisive blow to the enemy.

Toward the end of his letter General Arista stated:

I and all my subordinates are possessed of enthusiasm, in order to give the Anglo-Saxon race to understand that Mexico cannot be insulted with impunity.[7]

Indeed, just as generals Pedro de Ampudia and Mariano Arista had contemplated, General Anastasio Torrejón was the one to initiate the war. On April 25, 1846, on the left (Texan) bank of the Rio Grande, General Torrejón, with 1600 cavalry troops, attacked Captain Seth Thornton, who commanded a scouting party of sixty-three American dragoons. The Mexican war had now begun.

In the first six chapters our focus was on Texas. It was shown that Texas indeed established its independence from Mexico and that the Rio Grande served as the Mexican-Texas frontier.

In the second part of this book thus far, the emphasis has been on Mexican-American relations. What has come to light as a result of this investigation is the constant theme of Mexican threats contrasted with American peaceful endeavors.

Chapter 12 speaks for itself. Here the Mexicans are revealed as plotting the war they had previously threatened.

As a result of this inquiry it is hoped that history will place the cause of the Mexican War where it rightly belongs: on the Mexican military, who first provoked the Texans into independence, then by continued harassment drove Texas into the arms of the

[7]In Paredes Papers, Wallet 145, number 242.

147

United States, and finally invaded what had become American territory.

This author has come to the further conclusion that the Mexican military, unwilling to admit in their arrogant pride that a handful of Texans had defeated them, continued to bury their heads in the sand and proclaim that Texas was a "department" of Mexico, while in truth it was merely a department of their self-created fantasy. Having incited their own people to expect the subjugation of Texas, the Mexican military were unable to dismount the tiger of their own illusions when this prospect became totally unattainable as a result of the American annexation of Texas.

Blinded by their own propaganda, Mexican generals could retain the presidential palace only as long as they advocated the impossible: the conquest of Texas. When General José Joaquín de Herrera appeared to waver in this determination by allowing an American envoy, John Slidell, even to land in Mexico to discuss a peaceful solution to the question of Texas, he was overthrown by the more militant General Mariano Paredes y Arrillaga.

Unfortunately for the Mexican braggarts in uniform, President Polk took their threats seriously enough to send United States units to the frontiers. With the appearance of General Zachary Taylor in the vicinity of the Rio Grande and of Commodores David Conner, Robert F. Stockton, and John D. Sloat in the waters off the coast of Mexico, the Mexican braggadocio had run full course.

It fell to General Mariano Paredes y Arrillaga, then serving as president of Mexico, either to admit the inadmissible—the loss of Texas—or to initiate war. Actually, General Paredes had little choice. To expose the previous Mexican threats as empty gestures and accept a peaceful solution that would concede the loss of Texas would have been to invite his own overthrow by yet another military chieftain who would have promised to evict the *gringos* from the "soil of Mexico."

The time had arrived for the Mexican military, now personified in General Mariano Paredes y Arrillaga, to fish or cut bait. General Paredes chose to fish in the dangerous waters of the Rio Grande.

Epilogue
A Brief Summary of the War

Having attacked the Americans on the Texan side of the Rio Grande on April 25, 1846, the Mexicans began moving larger forces across that river during the period of April 30 to May 1.

General Zachary Taylor hastened the construction of defenses at Point Isabel, on the Gulf Coast just north of the Rio Grande. General Taylor then marched his 2300 troops to relieve a small force of Americans at Fort Texas, located directly on the border within sight of the Rio Grande.

On May 8, near the Palo Alto water hole and still north of the Rio Grande, General Taylor encountered 6000 Mexican troops under General Mariano Arista. In the ensuing battle of Palo Alto, General Taylor emerged the victor, the superior fire of the American guns having defeated the larger Mexican army. American losses were 9 killed and 45 wounded. Mexican casualties are estimated at between 300 and 400.

General Arista, retreating southward, stopped at a ravine called Resaca de Guerrero. General Taylor, however, continued pursuit without awaiting reinforcements. On the following day, May 9, the Americans occupied the nearby ravine of Resaca de la Palma. This time Taylor's force was down to 1700 effective troops, while the Mexicans now numbered 5700. Again General Taylor defeated General Arista. American losses at the battle of Resaca de la Palma were 39 killed and 83 wounded; estimated Mexican casualties were 262 killed, 355 wounded, and about 150 captured or missing. Many other Mexicans drowned in their attempt to flee across the Rio Grande.

On the evening of May 9, the Mexicans abandoned the seige of Fort Texas, which was renamed Fort Brown in honor of the commanding officer who had defended the stronghold. Just across the Rio Grande from Fort Brown, General Mariano Arista evacuated the stronghold of Matamoros on May 17-18. On the 18th, General Taylor crossed the Rio Grande and occupied Matamoros. General Mariano Arista, having been twice defeated by the Americans, left the task of halting Taylor's advance to General Pedro de Ampudia. In the subsequent battle of Monterey, September 20–24, 1846, General Taylor, with 6000 men, defeated 10,000 Mexicans under General Ampudia.

General Taylor's front in northern Mexico was now to remain relatively quiet until February 22–23, 1847, when he achieved his great triumph at Buena Vista and thus ended the war in northern Mexico. Taylor lost 267 killed, 456 wounded, and 23 missing from an initial force of about 4800 men. The Mexican general whom Taylor defeated at Buena Vista was Antonio López de Santa Anna, who had only recently returned from exile. General Santa Anna's forces, which had numbered over 15,000 troops, suffered a 10 per cent loss: 1500 casualties, of which at least 500 were killed.

In the western or California section of the fighting, events also went well for the United States. A revolt of the Californians, known as the Bear Flag Revolt and lasting from June 10 to July 5, 1846, blended into victories achieved under the command of General Stephen Watts Kearny, and California was soon under the Stars and Stripes.

The major American victories, however, were to go to General Winfield Scott, whose Vera Cruz Expedition of February 21-March 29, 1847 successfully placed American troops in a position to march on Mexico City itself. General Scott won a series of victories: Cerro Gordo, April 28; Contreras, August

19-20; and Churubusco, August 20. In these engagements General Scott's troops never numbered more than 10,000. Scott's adversary was the perennial General Antonio López de Santa Anna, newly installed as president of Mexico despite his defeat at Buena Vista by General Zachary Taylor.

With the failure of early peace negotiations, the armistice of Tacubaya, lasting from August 24 to September 7, 1847, collapsed, and General Scott headed for Mexico City. Before taking the capital, however, General Scott decided to storm the hill of Chapultepec, commanding the causeways leading to the gates of Mexico City.

The 15,000 Mexican troops under President Santa Anna were no match for General Winfield Scott's 7180 Americans. When the two-day battle ended on September 13, 1847, the United States army controlled Chapultepec hill. General Scott immediately pressed into the Mexican capital on the night of September 13-14.

General Santa Anna, defeated in the Mexican heartland, fled to the suburb of Guadalupe Hidalgo. Here, on September 16 he resigned the presidency. On October 7 Santa Anna was deposed as head of the Mexican army, and he fled the country.

While the fighting was going on, President Polk sent a confidential agent, Nicholas P. Trist, to Mexico to seek a permanent peace. The Trist mission ultimately resulted in the Treaty of Guadalupe Hidalgo of February 2, 1848. Under this treaty the Mexicans surrendered their pretentions to Texas as well as to the entire Southwest all the way to California.

President Polk's victory in a war he had hoped to avoid, however, was paid for by losses in domestic politics, just as he had feared. General Zachary Taylor, emerging as a war hero, was named by the opposition Whig party as its presidential candidate in 1848 and went on to win the election.

Thus ended a chapter in American history with the torch of liberty and democratic government waving uninterruptedly from the Atlantic to the Pacific.

Bibliography

Selected Primary Sources

1. Manuscripts

Jones, Anson. *Anson Jones Papers*, University of Texas Archives, Barker History Center, Austin, Texas.

Lamar, Mirabeau B. *Mirabeau B. Lamar Papers*, University of Texas Archives, Barker History Center, Austin, Texas.

Paredes y Arrillaga, Mariano. *Mariano Paredes y Arrillaga Papers*, García Collection, University of Texas Archives, Latin American Collection, Austin, Texas.

2. Government Documents

Mexico. Executive Document. *Ultimas Comunicaciónes entre el Gobierno Mexicano y el enviado estraórdinario y ministro plenipoteniario nombrado por el de los Estados Unidos, sobre la Cuestion De Tejas, y admision de dicho agente.* Mexico City: Imprenta de Ignacio Cumplido, 1846.

Texas. *Executive Department Journals.*

United States Congress. *The Congressional Globe.*

United States Congress, House of Representatives. *Executive Documents.*

United States Congress, Senate. *Executive Documents.*

3. Printed Materials.

Adams, Ephraim Douglass [Ed.], *British Diplomatic Correspondence Concerning The Republic of Texas–1838-1846.* Austin: Texas State Historical Association, 1917.

Barker, Eugene C. [Ed.], *The Austin Papers,* 3 vols. Washington: Government Printing Office, 1924-1928.

Binkley, William C. [Ed.], *Official Correspondence of the Texan Revolution,* 2 vols. New York: Vanderbilt Univ., 1936.

Bosch García, Carlos [Ed.], *Materia para la Historia Diplomática de México (México y los Estados Unidos, 1820–1848).* Mexico City: Universidad Nacional Autónoma de México, 1957.

Filisola, Vicente. *Memorias para la historia de la Guerra de Tejas.* Mexico City: Imprenta de Ignacio Cumplido, 1849.

Filisola, Vicente. *Evacuation of Texas.* (Translation of the Representation Addressed to the Supreme Government by General Vicente Filisola in defense of his honor, August 19, 1836. Translated by George Louis Hammeken in 1837. Edited by James M. Day in 1965). Waco, Tex.: Texian Press, 1965.

Jones, Anson. *Memoranda and Official Correspondence relating to the Republic Of Texas, its History And Annexation.* New York: Appleton, 1859.

Manning, William R. [Ed.], *Diplomatic Correspondence of the United States,* vol. VIII (1860). Washington: Carnegie Endowment for International Peace, 1937.

Paredes y Arrillaga, Mariano. *La Situación Política, Militar, y Económica en la República Mexicana al iniciarse su guerra con los Estados Unidos.* Edited by Genaro García. Mexico City: Ignacio B. Del Castillo, 1913.

Polk, James Knox. *The Diary of James K. Polk during his Presidency, 1845-1849.* Edited by Milo Milton Quaife. Chicago: McClurg, 1910.

Richardson, James D. [Ed.], *A Compilation of the Messages and Papers of the Presidents,* vol. VI. New York: Bureau of National Literature, 1897. vol. IV. Washington: Government Printing Office, 1897. (20 vol. series, printed by two separate publishers).

Santa Anna, Antonio López de. *Mi Historia Militar y Política, 1810-1879; Memorias Inéditas.* Mexico City: Editorial Nacional, 1958. Originally published by Genaro García and Carlos Pereyra in 1905.

Tarnava, Constantino. Letter to Lucas Alamán, Jan. 14, 1830, University of Texas Transcripts (from the Department of Fomento, Mexico, legajo 5, expediente 30), Barker History Center, Austin, Texas.

Wallace, Ernest, & Vignes, David M. [Eds.], *Documents of Texas History*. Austin: Steck, 1960 (1963 edition).

4. Newspapers

El Cosmopolita (Mexico City).

New Orleans *Bee*.

New Orleans *Union*.

Niles' National Register (Baltimore).

Telegraph and Texas Register (San Felipe and Columbia, pre-1837; Houston, 1837-1846).

Texas Republican (Brazoria).

Washington *Globe*.

Selected Secondary Sources

Adams, Ephraim Douglass, "English Interest in the Annexation of California," *The American Historical Review*, XIV, no. 4 (July 1909).

Adams, Ephraim Douglass, *British Interests and Activities in Texas, 1836-1846*. Gloucester, Mass.: Peter Smith, 1963.

Barker, Eugene C., *The Life of Stephen F. Austin, Founder of Texas, 1793-1836*. Dallas: Cokesbury Press, 1926.

Barker, Eugene C. *Mexico and Texas, 1821-1835*. New York: Russell & Russell, 1965 (originally published in 1928).

Binkley, William C., *The Texas Revolution*. Baton Rouge: Louisiana State University Press, 1952.

Boucher, Chauncey W., "In Re That Aggressive Slaveocracy," *Mississippi Valley Historical Review*, VIII (1921).

Estep, Raymond, *Lorenzo de Zavala: Profeta del Liberalismo Mexicano*. Mexico City: Librería de Manuel Porrua, 1952.

Nance, Joseph Milton, *After San Jacinto: The Texas-Mexican Frontier, 1836-1841*. Austin: University of Texas Press, 1963.

Nance, Joseph Milton, *Attack and Counter-Attack: The Texas-Mexican Frontier, 1842*. Austin: University of Texas Press, 1964.

Reeves, Jesse R., *American Diplomacy under Tyler and Polk*. Baltimore: Johns Hopkins Press, 1907.

Rives, George Lockhart, *The United States and Mexico: 1821-1848*. New York: Scribner's, 1913.

Smith, Justin Harvey, *The Annexation of Texas*. New York: Macmillan, 1941 (corrected ed.; originally published by Baker, 1911.)

Smith, Justin Harvey, *The War with Mexico*. New York: Macmillan, 1919.

Toro, Alfonso. *Compendio de Historia de México*. Mexico City: Editorial Patria, S.A., 1956 (8th ed.).

Vasconcelos, José, *Breve Historia de México, Edición Contemporánea,* Mexico City: Cia Editorial Continental, S.A., 1959 (4th ed.; 1st ed. in 1956).

Index

160